INVESTING
FOR TEENS

How to Build Wealth Before 20—
Even If You're Starting with

by

EVAN SIMMONS

Investing for Teens : How to Build Wealth
Before 20—Even If You're Starting with

TABLE OF CONTENTS

INTRODUCTION

Money can feel like a mysterious force—sometimes it's thrilling, other times it feels confusing or out of reach. For many teens, money management and investing might seem like topics only adults deal with, or maybe things for "rich people" to worry about. But that's far from the truth. In fact, the earlier you start learning about money and investing, the more control you'll have over your financial future. This book is designed to help you get comfortable with money in a way that fits your life, your goals, and your level of experience.

Think of this as your financial toolkit, packed with ideas and advice that don't just sound smart but actually work when you put them into action. You'll hear practical tips on how to handle your money daily, and you'll also learn how to grow it over time. You might already know a little about saving your allowance or birthday cash, but here's the exciting part—you're about to discover how to make your money work for you instead of just sitting in a jar or spending as soon as you get it. This shift in mindset is huge.

As a teenager, you're in a prime spot to build habits that can set you up for lifelong financial confidence. The habits and choices you make now don't just shape your bank account tomorrow—they shape the kind of life and freedom you'll enjoy down the road. Maybe you want the freedom to travel, start a business, go to college without massive debt, or even retire early someday. It all starts with learning the basics and then putting that knowledge into practice.

One thing you'll notice right away is that money management isn't just about math or budgets—it's about understanding your goals and values. What matters most to you? Are you saving to buy a car, fund a college trip, or maybe even launch your own startup? Whatever you want, mastering money helps you get there faster and smarter. This book doesn't judge your goals; it helps you reach them.

It's also normal to feel overwhelmed or unsure about where to start, especially when you hear words like "stocks," "compounding," or "investment portfolio." Don't worry— that's exactly why this guide breaks things down into easy, bite-sized pieces tailored just for teens. Nothing boring, nothing too complicated, just clear explanations and real-life examples you can relate to. By the time you finish the chapters ahead, the terms that once felt like a language barrier will seem second nature.

Another important idea here is that building wealth isn't about quick wins or easy money. It's about patience, learning from mistakes, and sticking with smart strategies even when it doesn't seem glamorous. Financial success is a journey with ups and downs, and this book will encourage you to think long-term. Starting early gives you a huge advantage, thanks to time and the power of compound growth, but it really takes consistent effort to see big results.

While we'll talk a lot about how to earn and invest money, it's equally about the way you think about money. Your mindset can either be your biggest asset or your biggest obstacle. Learning to think like an investor means making choices that align with your future rather than just your immediate wants. Whether it's saying no to impulse buys or standing firm when friends make risky spending decisions, these mental moves are just as crucial as any tip about stocks or savings accounts.

Though money matters might sound serious, you'll find that managing your finances and investing can be creative and even fun once you start understanding how all the pieces fit together. For example, you might discover how side hustles can boost your saving power, or how to spot warning signs of scams and false promises. You'll realize how being financially savvy helps you take better control over your life—not just your wallet.

This isn't just another textbook. It's a guide written with teenagers in mind—your pace, your language, your challenges. It respects that you're balancing school, friendships, hobbies, and figuring out who you are. The ideas you'll learn here are meant to fit into your busy life and grow with you as you mature. You don't have to be perfect or have tons of money to start. Every small step counts, and this book will show you how to take those first smart steps confidently.

Over the coming chapters, you'll explore essential money basics like setting goals, budgeting in ways that actually work, and the real difference between saving and investing. You'll get clear, simple guides to understanding investing, breaking down complex topics with straightforward language and relatable examples. Plus, you'll learn how to start investing even if you don't have hundreds or thousands of dollars right now.

Along the way, you'll also discover the importance of developing the right habits and mindset to stay on track despite challenges or peer pressure. We'll cover how to avoid common traps like scams and hype from social media "gurus," how to keep your motivation steady, and how to make money through side hustles that fit your skills and schedule. These ideas will prepare you not just to grow wealth but to protect it too.

Finally, this book will help you see the bigger picture—looking beyond just teen years and into your future as an adult. We'll talk about building a portfolio that grows with you, strategies to handle market ups and downs, and what financial freedom really means. This part is about empowering you to make thoughtful decisions and set a roadmap for your 20s, 30s, and the decades ahead.

Getting smart about money right now might feel like a challenge, but it can also be one of the most rewarding things you ever do. Imagine the confidence that comes with knowing you have control over your financial life, the skills to grow your money responsibly, and the experience to avoid common pitfalls. That confidence can open doors to opportunities others might miss.

There's no single "right" way to manage money or invest, but there are plenty of proven strategies that work well, especially when you start early and stay consistent. You'll develop your own plan and style as you go along, but this book will make sure you start with a solid foundation.

Your financial journey starts here. By diving into these pages, you're already ahead of many adults who wish they had learned these lessons sooner. So, let's get started and take control of your money, your future, and the freedom that comes with it.

CHAPTER 1

MONEY BASICS EVERY TEEN NEEDS

Understanding money isn't just about counting cash or knowing how to spend it; it's about grasping the habits and principles that set you up for financial freedom later in life. Most schools don't teach how to actually manage, save, or grow money, but those skills are the keys to unlocking opportunities down the road. This chapter covers essential concepts like why budgeting doesn't have to be boring, how to set meaningful financial goals that actually motivate you, and the crucial difference between saving money safely and investing it to make it work harder. Grasping these basics will give you a strong foundation to build smarter money habits and get ready for investing with confidence, no matter where you start.

MONEY 101: WHAT THEY DIDN'T TEACH YOU IN SCHOOL

It's strange how school teaches you about calculus, history, and literature, but never explains the basics of money—the one thing you'll use every day for the rest of your life. If you're like most teens, you probably learned about money from your parents, friends, or maybe even social media influencers. But guess what? There's a lot that they leave out, and that's where this section comes in. We're going to pull back the curtain on some money truths that most classrooms skip, so you don't have to stumble through real life figuring them out on your own.

First off, let's talk about what money really is. It's not just about coins, bills, or numbers in a bank account. Money is a tool—a powerful one—that lets you trade your time, skills, or goods for things you want or need. Understanding that mindset changes everything. Money isn't something to fear or obsess over; it's something to control and use wisely. It's kind of like a smartphone. When you know how to use it well, it makes life easier. If you misuse it or ignore it, you end up missing out or creating stress for yourself.

One of the biggest lessons school often misses is that money doesn't grow on trees, but it sure can grow if you treat it right. The idea of making your money work for you sounds almost magical, but it's real—more real than most people get in their 20s, 30s, or even 40s. When you start early, you give your money time to multiply quietly, often without you even noticing at first. That's why learning about

14

money in your teenage years isn't just helpful—it's a game changer.

Another tricky thing that school tends to ignore is how complicated money rules can be—like taxes, fees, interest rates, credit scores, and budgeting. These aren't the most thrilling topics, but they're super important. Little things like understanding how credit cards work or the consequences of borrowing money can save you from huge headaches down the road. And speaking of credit cards, many adults don't even fully get how they work, so it's no wonder teens don't get taught about them! Knowing this stuff early means you won't fall into traps that take years to climb out of.

Now, imagine if someone had told you when you were 13 that saving even a couple of dollars a week could turn into thousands by the time you're in your 20s. You might have thought, "No way, that sounds boring." But that's the power of compound interest, and it's the kind of financial superpower that almost no one teaches you in traditional schools. Starting early means your money has years to grow, like planting a tree when it's a sapling instead of trying to grow it when it's already huge. The earlier you start, the more effortless your money's growth can be.

Besides the basics of saving and spending, there's the whole idea of financial mindset, which is almost never discussed in classrooms. How you think about money shapes how you handle it. Do you see money as a limited resource you have to hoard or a tool to build your dreams? Developing healthy money habits now, like tracking where your money goes, setting goals, and being mindful about wants versus needs, sets you up for real success.

One common myth that needs busting is that investing is only for rich people or adults. In reality, investing is for anyone who wants to grow their money, including teens. School might skip this because investing sounds complex or risky, but when you break it down, it's just a way to put your money into something that might earn more money over time. The sooner you understand this, the more confident you'll feel about your financial future.

Speaking of risks, schools rarely teach how to manage money risks. They focus on formulas and facts but rarely on personal decision-making's emotional side. Money decisions often come with risks and rewards, and learning how to balance these is crucial. For example, it's smart to know when to save for something safe and when to take a chance on an investment that could pay off bigger later. Recognizing your comfort with risk—and how it fits with your goals—is part of real-world money smarts that school doesn't cover.

And don't forget about the traps! There are plenty of money mistakes people make that you can avoid if you know what to watch out for. From payday loans charging insane interest rates to scams promising quick riches, being financially savvy means knowing which offers and opportunities are legit and which ones are riskier than they sound. Schools usually don't prepare you to spot these, so it's something you'll have to learn outside class.

16

Another part of the "missing lessons" is understanding that money isn't just about you. A lot of people forget how much financial choices impact relationships—family, friends, or partners. Communicating about money, sharing bills, and making joint money decisions can be tricky but vital to avoid conflicts and lifelong stress. This isn't something you'll see in textbooks, but it's real life and crucial for a healthy future.

When you start paying attention to money on your own terms, you realize it's not something to be scared of. It's a skill like learning sports or music. Nobody becomes a pro overnight, but with practice and patience, you get better and better. The confidence that comes from understanding money basics will ripple into other parts of your life. You'll be able to make decisions about college, jobs, and independence with clarity instead of confusion or stress.

How you use money today shapes your future freedom. Picture your money as a muscle. The more you exercise it through smart saving, budgeting, and investing, the stronger your financial life will be. That strength means you'll have options down the line—maybe traveling, starting a business, or just living without constant money worries. But it all begins with knowing the basics that, surprisingly, school never touches.

Let's finish by reminding you that no one is born knowing how to handle money. Even adults screw it up sometimes. The important part is starting now, making mistakes, learning, and improving bit by bit. The knowledge you pick up today will set you apart from most people your age and give you a huge advantage as you move toward financial independence and wealth. So consider this section your financial wake-up call: don't wait for someone else to teach you what really matters about money. Take control and build your future with intention.

HOW TO SET SMART FINANCIAL GOALS EVERY TEEN SHOULD KNOW

Setting financial goals might sound like a boring chore — something adults talk about at the kitchen table — but it's actually one of the most powerful ways for teens to take control of their money and build real wealth over time. Without clear goals, money might just slip through your fingers like water. But when you set goals the SMART way, you give yourself a roadmap that actually works, helping you focus on what matters and stay motivated even when things get tricky.

SMART is an acronym that stands for Specific, Measurable, Achievable, Relevant, and Time-bound. These five criteria shape your financial goals so they're clear and realistic. It's easy to say "I want to save money," but much harder (and way more effective) to say, "I want to save $500 in the next six months so I can buy a laptop." The first version is too vague; the second one is an actual SMART goal.

Let's break each part down to see how this works in real life for teens:

1. **Specific:** Vague goals don't lead to action. Saying "I want to save money" is helpful, but not enough to build a plan. Instead, get specific. Ask yourself: What exactly am I saving for? Is it a new phone, a car, a trip? The clearer the goal, the easier it is to picture success and decide what steps to take.

2. **Measurable:** You need a way to measure progress. Saying "I want to be better with money" doesn't give you a way to track if you're winning or losing. But saying "I want to save $300 in three months" lets you check your progress weekly or monthly. It's like keeping score in a game; you want to know if you're moving closer to the finish line.

3. **Achievable:** It's also important your goal feels possible. Saving $5,000 in a month when you get $20 a week in allowance might set you up for disappointment. Pick goals that challenge you but are doable with effort. That way, when you achieve them, it boosts your confidence and keeps you pushing forward.

4. **Relevant:** Your money goals should matter to you—not your parents, friends, or anyone else. If you're not excited about the goal, you're less likely to stick with it. Maybe buying your first car feels more motivating than saving for a fancy gadget.

Align your goal with what really matters in your life.

5. **Time-bound:** Without a deadline, goals tend to drag on forever without action. Saying "I'll save $1,000 someday" can stretch into never-land. But "I will save $1,000 in 10 months" creates urgency. Deadlines help you prioritize and make consistent progress.

Imagine you want to buy a bike. Instead of blurting out, "I want a bike," try this SMART goal: "I will save $250 in five months to buy a mountain bike." It's specific (a mountain bike), measurable ($250), achievable (is $50 a month realistic for you?), relevant (you want it for fun or transportation), and time-bound (five months). Now you've got a clear target to aim for.

Once you write down your goals, the next step is to break them into smaller chunks. Saving $250 might feel intimidating, but when you divide that by five months, it's just $50 a month. Better yet, break the $50 into weekly amounts—about $12.50 per week—and suddenly, the goal feels doable, even if you don't have a huge allowance or income yet. Consider it like leveling up in a video game; small wins lead to bigger victories.

Writing your goals in a journal or a dedicated app can help you stay accountable. When you see your progress, even small deposits into your savings account feel like victories. Celebrate those wins! Building good habits is just as important as the numbers themselves, and feeling proud keeps motivation high.

Another important piece? Make sure your goals aren't in conflict with each other. Trying to save for a phone and also spend big on clothes might stretch your budget thin. Prioritize. Which goal excites you most? Or are you able to work on multiple goals at once, maybe by balancing saving and spending? Think about how your money moves and make a plan that fits your lifestyle.

Setting SMART goals isn't just about saving money; it's also a crucial skill for investing, which we'll dive into later. When you pick an investment, you're kind of setting a financial goal too—for example, "I want to grow $500 into $700 in a year." Goals give you direction, and direction is everything when it comes to making smart money moves.

Some teens might worry that setting goals means giving up fun spending or freedom. But actually, SMART goals help you spend intentionally. Instead of mindlessly blowing cash on random things, you learn how to balance enjoyment with responsibility. It's about creating a lifestyle where you can have both fun and long-term security.

It's worth mentioning that life throws curveballs, so don't freak out if you miss a goal. Goals aren't set in stone— they're tools to help guide you. Adjust your timeline or your amounts as needed. What matters most is that you keep moving forward and don't give up just because things got tough. Learning from setbacks is part of the process.

Ready to put this into practice? Start by choosing one financial goal. Take a moment to think—what's that one thing you want most right now that requires money? Is it saving for a concert, a new phone, or maybe to start investing? Write it down on paper or on your phone, then make it SMART. Define each piece, make sure it fits your timeline, and break it into smaller steps.

Then, track your progress weekly. Seeing how close you're getting creates momentum. And remember, each dollar you save or invest is like planting a seed for your future. It might not look like much at first, but with time and consistency, those seeds grow into something amazing.

Financial goals might seem like a grown-up thing, but the truth is, they give you amazing control over your future. When you master how to set SMART financial goals today, you're not just managing money—you're shaping your dreams into reality. And that's way cooler than just hoping things will work out.

BUDGETING WITHOUT BOREDOM: KEEP MORE, WASTE LESS TIPS FOR TEENS

Budgeting might sound like a chore—something boring adults do to keep their lives "in order." But, honestly, it doesn't have to be dull or frustrating. For teens, budgeting is actually a powerful tool that helps you control your money rather than letting money control you. When you master budgeting early, you're setting yourself up for real financial freedom later on. Plus, it means you get to keep more of your cash and waste less on stuff that doesn't really matter. This section is all about making budgeting fun, practical, and easy to stick with.

First off, the key to avoiding boredom in budgeting is all about keeping it simple and relatable. Forget those complicated spreadsheets with endless rows of numbers. Start small, maybe with a notebook, an app on your phone, or even a plain piece of paper. Write down your money coming in—like allowance, payments from jobs, or birthday cash—and your money going out, whether it's snacks, apps, or that new pair of sneakers you're eyeing. The goal isn't to get super detailed right away but to get a clear picture of where your money is actually going. Once you see it on paper, it becomes easier to spot what you can cut back on.

One smart trick to keep your budget from feeling like a drag is to turn it into a game. Challenge yourself to spend less on certain categories each week or month and reward yourself when you meet those goals. For example, if you usually spend $20 a week on snacks, try cutting it down to $10. Put the $10 you saved into your savings jar or account and watch how quickly it grows. This kind of challenge keeps budgeting active and shows how small changes add up. It's also a great way to boost your motivation because you'll actually see progress without feeling deprived.

It's super important to build room for fun in your budget. Budgeting isn't about cutting out everything you enjoy—it's about balance. Saving all your money without enjoying any of it isn't sustainable or enjoyable. So, make sure you carve out a "fun fund" just for things you like, whether it's going to the movies, buying that cool game, or hanging out with friends. When you know there's money earmarked specifically for fun, you won't feel guilty when you spend it. Plus, this stops impulsive splurges on random things because you're sticking to a plan where fun has its own spot.

Another huge tip for teens is to embrace the "pay yourself first" mindset. That means before spending money on anything else, put aside a portion for saving and investing. This is one of the simplest but smartest moves you can make. Imagine getting your paycheck, taking out $10 or $20 straight away and dropping it into your savings or investment account, then living off what's left. Doing this regularly helps build wealth over time and makes saving a habit rather than an afterthought. The best part? Once your savings grow, it gives you more control to spend or invest without feeling stressed about it.

Keeping track of your spending doesn't mean you have to be boring or too rigid. Use technology to your advantage by downloading teen-friendly budgeting apps. These apps can sync with your accounts, categorize your expenses automatically, and send reminders to keep you on track. A lot of them have fun features like badges, progress bars, or social sharing to keep you motivated. If apps aren't your thing, even setting alarms or calendar reminders to check your budget regularly can help keep you accountable.

When cutting costs, it's easy to think about depriving yourself or making huge sacrifices. But waste less doesn't mean life has to be dull. Start by being mindful about small purchases. For example, those daily $2 coffees add up quickly—over a month, that's at least $60! Instead of buying coffee every day, maybe make it at home a few times a week or switch it up with water or tea. It's these tiny hacks that help you keep more money over time without feeling like you're missing out.

Another idea: get creative with ways to save on everyday expenses. Think about swapping clothes with friends instead of always buying new ones, cooking your meals instead of eating out, or even hunting for free or low-cost entertainment options like local events, museums, or hikes. Being resourceful turns budgeting from a boring task into a fun challenge to see how much you can save while still living your best life.

Sometimes peer pressure and social media can push us to spend more than we should. You might see friends buying the newest gadget or trendy clothes and feel like you have to keep up. But remember, budgeting means making choices that work for your goals, not someone else's. Instead of spending to fit in, try finding ways to enjoy your social life without breaking the bank. Host game nights, picnic in the park, or watch movies at home. These low-cost hangouts keep friendships strong and your wallet healthy at the same time.

Another inspiring part of budgeting is learning to say "no" when you really need to. It's hard sometimes, especially if your friends are spending or if there's a new must-have release, but saying no sometimes is a powerful act of self-control. When you say no, you're choosing your financial future over instant gratification. Trust me, your future self will thank you when you have money saved and aren't in debt just because you couldn't pass up a few trendy items or extra nights out.

Budgeting can also teach you some essential life skills beyond just saving money. It helps you become more organized, responsible, and intentional about your decisions. These skills will come in handy as your money—and life—gets more complex. You'll be able to handle college costs, car expenses, and eventually rent or mortgages with confidence. Starting early with budgeting without boredom sets the foundation for financial confidence that lasts a lifetime.

It's important to remember the mindset around budgeting matters a lot. If you think of it as punishment or a strict rulebook, you'll resist it. But if you embrace budgeting as a way to create choices and freedom, it becomes empowering. Every dollar you save is a step closer to the things that really matter to you, whether that's a car, college, a trip, or investing to build your wealth. When you control your money instead of letting it control you, you unlock options and reduce stress.

Finally, don't be afraid of adjusting your budget over time. Life changes fast, especially as a teen. Your income might grow with new jobs, your wants and needs will change, and unexpected expenses will pop up. Budgeting isn't set in stone—it's a flexible plan that evolves. Review your budget regularly and tweak it to fit where you are. This way, it stays relevant and keeps empowering you rather than becoming a drag.

In the end, budgeting without boredom is all about keeping it real, fun, and focused on your goals. It's a skill you can make your own with a little creativity and mindset shift. As you start getting into the habit, remember that every dollar you save is money you keep and power you gain. That's the kind of financial freedom every teen deserves.

SAVING VS. INVESTING: KNOW THE DIFFERENCE, MASTER BOTH FOR YOUR FUTURE

When it comes to money, you've probably heard the words "saving" and "investing" thrown around a lot. They might seem like the same thing at first — both involve putting money aside for future use — but they're actually quite different. Understanding how each works and why you need both will set you up for a strong financial future. Saving and investing are two sides of the same coin, but they serve different purposes in your money game.

Let's start with saving. Saving is all about keeping your money safe and accessible. Think of it like putting cash into a piggy bank or a savings account at the bank. The main goal with saving is to have money ready when you need it, without risking losing any of it. Saving is perfect for short-term goals, like buying a new phone, covering an emergency expense, or even saving for a concert ticket next month. It's the money you don't want to touch right now, but might need soon.

Since your focus with saving is security, the growth on your money is slow, often barely beating inflation. This means while you don't lose money in savings, it also won't multiply quickly. Savings accounts usually offer low interest rates, which is fine because the priority is preserving your money, not growing it fast. Having a solid savings cushion is a financial safety net — it's what keeps you out of trouble when things don't go as planned.

Investing, on the other hand, is about putting your money to work with the goal of building wealth over time. When you invest, you're essentially buying pieces of companies (stocks), lending money to governments or businesses (bonds), or buying ownership in other assets. Investing is riskier than saving because the value of what you buy can go up and down, sometimes dramatically. But that risk comes with the potential for much bigger rewards.

Why risk your money? Because investing allows your money to grow faster than it would just sitting in a savings account. Over the long run, markets generally trend upward, which means if you invest wisely and stay consistent, your money can multiply significantly. This growth can set the stage for major goals like buying a car, funding college, or even starting your own business someday.

Your age as a teen is actually a huge advantage when it comes to investing. Time is one of the best allies investors have because of the power of compounding — where your investment earnings start to make even more money for you. This snowball effect means the earlier you start investing, the more time your money has to grow, turning what starts as a small amount into something much bigger.

That doesn't mean you should avoid saving altogether. Think about saving and investing as working together rather than separately. You need a balance. The first step is usually to build an emergency fund — money saved in an account you can access easily if something unexpected happens. It's your financial shield, so you don't have to quickly pull out investments, which might be down in value at that moment.

Once you have that safety net, it's easier to invest with confidence. You won't feel pressured to sell your stocks or investments if the market goes through a rough patch because you know your immediate needs are covered by your savings. This mental space allows your investments the time they deserve to grow and recover.

Another key difference between saving and investing is your mindset around risk and reward. Saving is low risk, low reward, like playing it safe in a game just to stay in. Investing is high risk, high reward, where you're willing to take some chances because the payoff can be huge down the road. The trick is figuring out how much risk you're comfortable with, which comes with learning about different types of investments and understanding how volatility affects your money.

For many teens, the challenge is figuring out how to split their money between saving and investing. There's no one-size-fits-all answer. It depends on your goals, your financial situation, and your personality. If you're saving for a big purchase coming up soon, like a laptop or car, putting that money in a high-yield savings account or certificate of deposit (CD) makes sense. But if you're thinking about building wealth for college or your 20s, investing a portion of your money in stocks, bonds, or mutual funds could pay off much more.

Remember, investing isn't only for people with a ton of money. Even with small amounts, you can start investing today. Many apps and platforms are designed specifically for teens and beginners, making it easier than ever to buy a fraction of a share or put money into an index fund. The important part is getting started and learning as you go. Like any skill, investing is about practice and patience.

Also, saving doesn't just mean sticking your money under your mattress or letting it sit idle. Putting your savings in accounts that offer some interest, even if it's just a little, helps your money grow somewhat while remaining safe. On the flip side, don't think investing is a shortcut to instant riches. It's a long-term game that requires research, discipline, and keeping emotions in check. Markets will have ups and downs, and staying calm during those times is key.

So, what about both? Saving and investing together build a strong financial foundation. Saving gives you stability; investing helps you grow your wealth. By mastering both, you're not just preparing for tomorrow — you're setting yourself up to make your money work hard for you over many years.

Let's say you start by setting aside $50 a month. You might put $30 into your savings for immediate needs and emergencies, and $20 into an investment account. Over time, as your savings build up, you can shift more money toward investing to maximize growth. It's a balancing act that will change as your needs and goals evolve.

Finally, think of saving and investing as skills you develop to give you freedom and options in life. Whether it's paying for college, traveling, or buying your first car, understanding and using both tools gives you control over your financial future. You don't have to wait until you're an adult to start. Starting now, even with just a little money and a lot of curiosity, puts you miles ahead.

Mastering saving and investing isn't about avoiding risks or hoarding cash. It's about knowing when to play it safe and when to take smart chances. It's about using money as a tool to build the life you want. And the best time to start is right now.

CHAPTER 2

INVESTING MADE SIMPLE FOR TEENS

Investing might sound complicated or like something only adults with tons of money do, but the truth is, it's a powerful tool anyone can start using—even you. It's not about having a fortune from day one; it's about understanding how to make your money work for you over time, so you can grow your wealth while you're still in school or working your first job. Getting the basics down early gives you a huge advantage because time is on your side, and even small amounts count when you invest smartly. Think of investing as planting seeds—the earlier you plant, the bigger your financial garden can grow. This chapter will break down the core ideas you need to know to get started confidently, inspire you to take action, and show that building financial independence isn't some far-off dream but something within your reach right now.

What Is Investing—and Why It's Not Just for Rich People

When you hear the word "investing," you might automatically think it's something only wealthy adults or business experts do. Maybe you picture people in suits shouting on the trading floor or imagine you need thousands of dollars just to get started. Here's the truth: investing isn't an exclusive club for rich people. In fact, investing is simply the act of putting your money to work so it grows over time. It's one of the smartest moves you can make to build wealth—no matter how much money you start with.

Think about it this way: when you plant a seed and care for it, eventually it grows into a tree that produces fruit. Investing works just like that. You take some money—your seed—and invest it in things like stocks, bonds, or even small businesses. Over time, through something called "growth" or sometimes "interest," your original money can grow bigger all on its own. The key is starting early and letting your money have time to grow.

Now, why does everyone emphasize starting when you're young? It boils down to time and opportunity. The younger you are, the more years you have for your investments to grow. This growth happens through a powerful force called compound interest, which we'll talk about later. For teens, starting early isn't just a cool idea—it's a huge advantage that can turn modest amounts of money into a financial safety net or even a launchpad for your dreams.

You might be wondering, "But I don't have any money to invest. How can I start?" The good news is that you don't need tons of cash to begin. Many investment platforms today let you start with little money, sometimes even just $5 or $10. The important part is building the habit of saving and investing regularly. Remember, investing isn't about making a quick buck or trying to get rich overnight. It's about patience and playing the long game.

Let's also bust a big myth: investing is risky, right? Sure, there's always some risk when it comes to money, but risk doesn't mean gambling. Investing wisely means understanding what you're putting your money into and balancing potential rewards against possible losses. It's a skill you can learn and get better at over time. And starting early lets you take more chances because you have time to recover if things don't go perfectly.

Investing is not a secret tool only for adults with big paychecks. It's actually a way for anyone to take control of their financial future. You don't need a job making thousands of dollars or a degree in finance. What you do need is curiosity, some basic knowledge, and most importantly, a willingness to start—whether that's with pocket change or money earned from your first part-time job or side hustle.

Why should teens care about investing now? Because the earlier you begin, the more freedom you create for yourself later. Imagine this: instead of living paycheck to paycheck, you're building a network of investments that give you choices—like going to college without debt, starting a business, or traveling the world. Investing helps you take steps toward financial independence, which means you don't have to rely solely on a job or loans as you get older.

Plus, when you learn about investing as a teen, you develop money habits that set you apart. You start thinking about money in a new way—not just spending it, but making it grow. That mindset shift is powerful. It can give you confidence when you face real financial decisions as an adult. You'll be less intimidated by money talk and more prepared to handle opportunities and challenges alike.

Another reason investing isn't just for the wealthy: opportunities exist everywhere. Thanks to technology, you can invest online from your phone or computer. You don't have to meet with fancy advisors right away. There are apps and platforms designed especially for beginners that simplify the process and help you learn along the way. It's like having a coach in your pocket who guides you step-by-step.

So, what kinds of things can you invest in? While we'll explore that more later, here's a snapshot: stocks (which mean owning a tiny piece of a company), bonds (which are loans you make to governments or companies), and even funds that group lots of investments together. Each has its own level of risk and reward, and starting early gives you time to figure out what fits you best.

Remember, investing doesn't always mean "buying stuff." Sometimes it's investing in yourself—like learning new skills or gaining education that can increase your future earning potential. But in this book, we're focusing mainly

36

on financial investing because it's a tool anyone can use with just a bit of discipline and curiosity.

It helps to think of investing as planting the seeds for your future. You won't see overnight success, but with regular care—like saving money, choosing smart investments, and getting educated—you'll watch those seeds grow stronger and taller. Just like a tree that starts from a small nut, your investments can become something big that provides for you for years to come.

In the end, investing is a chance for teens to take control rather than feeling helpless about money. Instead of waiting until you're an adult with a big paycheck, you can start making choices now that set you up for long-term success. No matter your background, income, or experience, you have the power to grow your money smarter than most adults do.

Don't let the idea of investing intimidate you. It's a skill, not a secret. And everyone can learn. So start asking questions, explore simple ways to invest, and keep building your financial confidence. Your future self will thank you for getting started early and believing that investing is for you—not just for the "rich folks."

THE MAGIC OF COMPOUND INTEREST: YOUR SECRET WEAPON IN INVESTING

You've probably heard that saving money is important, but the real game-changer when it comes to building wealth isn't just saving—it's how your money grows over time through compound interest. This concept is like planting a tiny seed that grows into a huge tree, but instead of water and sunlight, the fuel is time and reinvested earnings. Compound interest is what can turn a small investment you make today into a much larger sum down the road, even if you barely add any more money after that.

Here's the thing: compound interest means you don't just earn interest on the money you originally invested, but you also earn interest on the interest already accumulated. Think of it as interest making money for itself. The earlier you start investing, the more time your money has to bounce off itself and build momentum. So even if you start with just a little bit, the longer you stay invested, the more powerful your growth becomes.

The power of this compounding effect might not feel all that thrilling the first year or two. After all, earning a couple of extra dollars might seem meh, especially when you're busy with school and friends. But fast forward 10, 20, or 30 years, and suddenly your money is working way harder for you than you ever imagined. Imagine you started investing $100 at age 15 and never touched it. Thanks to compound interest, by the time you're 45, you could be sitting on a pile much bigger than $1000 just from steady growth—without you doing anything else.

It surprises a lot of teens to realize that compound interest moves really slowly at first. That's why so many adults tell you "the earlier, the better." At first, it might feel like your money is stuck. But if you give it enough time, the numbers begin accelerating. Think of it like a snowball rolling down a hill. When it starts, it's tiny, but as it rolls, it picks up more snow and gets bigger faster and faster. Your money works exactly like that.

Let's break down how compound interest actually works with a simple example. Say you invest $500 earning 5% interest annually. After the first year, you'll get $25 in interest and have $525 total. The next year, the 5% interest isn't just on your original $500; it's on $525. That means you'll earn $26.25 in interest. Each year your interest grows slightly because it's based on a bigger number, which keeps increasing. Over time, this effect snowballs, pushing your balance higher and higher.

One thing that's important to keep in mind is that compound interest depends on three key factors: the amount you invest, the interest rate your investment yields, and most importantly—time. Time is your best friend here. The longer you keep letting your money compound, the less effort you have to put in later on. That's why starting to invest in your teens, even with modest amounts, is much better than waiting until your 30s or 40s.

Here's a cool truth: it's better to invest a small amount now and let compound interest do its magic over many years than to wait until you have more money later. It sounds backwards, but this simple principle is the foundation of building wealth. Time is one of the most valuable assets you have; it's the secret ingredient that multiplies your money practically on autopilot.

But compound interest isn't just about letting money grow; it's about commitment too. If you add money regularly, like every month or every paycheck, your investment's growth can explode. It's like adding more snow to that snowball rolling downhill—boosting its size on the way. Even small consistent contributions make a big impact over time, so hábito of regular investing, even if it's just $10 or $20 a month, will pay off huge in the long run.

The best part? Compound interest applies not only to banks and savings accounts but also to anywhere your money earns returns—stocks, bonds, mutual funds, and even certain retirement accounts. Some investments offer higher potential returns (but usually with higher risks), and others are safer but grow more slowly. Regardless of where you invest, compound interest works behind the scenes, pushing your money higher if you let it stay invested.

Learning about compound interest might feel like understanding some funky math, but it's really all about patience and consistency. Financial success isn't about quick wins or luck. It's about small, smart steps that build on each other—growing stronger and faster over years. If you internalize this, you'll start seeing investing as a long-term journey rather than a one-time gamble.

Here's something that might blow your mind: if you start investing just $50 a month at 7% annual return when you're 16, you could have over $200,000 by the time you're 65. If you wait until you're 26 to start investing, you'd need to invest over $100 a month to catch up. That ten-year delay can cost you tens of thousands of dollars you'll never make up. Time really is the silent champion here, and compound interest is the engine powering your financial future.

Some people think compound interest only happens if you keep your money in a savings account with low interest. But actually, the best way for most people to benefit from compound interest is by investing in assets that offer higher returns—like stocks and funds. Even though these investments can be riskier, the growth potential means your money likely compounds faster and stronger over time compared to a basic savings account.

There's no magic fairy dust involved in compound interest—just consistent investing and letting your money grow patiently. Every deposit you avoid spending today can become a building block of your wealth tomorrow. And with compound interest, your money starts to 'pay you back' by working for you round the clock, even when you're sleeping, studying, or hanging out with friends.

Also, don't confuse compound interest with simple interest. Simple interest means you only earn interest on your original amount, like earning $10 every year on $100, regardless of what's accumulated. Compound interest, on the other hand, earns you interest on your original money plus the interest you already made. That's why compound interest can create so much bigger gains over time.

To make the most of this secret weapon, you'll want to avoid pulling your money out too early. Taking money out frequently interrupts the compounding process and slows the growth. The goal is to let your investments sit and work for you. The longer they stay untouched, the greater the impact of compound interest. Patience is a key ingredient here.

Compound interest also rewards those who are curious and educated about investments. The better you understand your options—how different investments grow and how often they pay interest or dividends—the more you can tailor your plan to supercharge your growth. It's like choosing the right soil and fertilizer for your money tree.

In the end, the real "magic" of compound interest lies in combining small actions, smart choices, and time. If you start investing early, stay consistent, and let your money keep growing, you'll have a financial advantage most adults never get because they waited too long or didn't understand this compound interest concept.

Remember: you don't need to be wealthy to take advantage of compound interest. You just need to start. It's one of the best tools for anyone who wants to grow their money without relying on luck or get-rich-quick schemes. With compound interest on your side, you're setting up a future where your money works for you—not the other way around.

So, as you think about investing and your financial future, let compound interest be your favorite word. It's not just a boring finance term—it's your secret weapon to building real wealth, starting right now.

How the Stock Market Works in Teen Language

So, you've heard about the stock market, right? It's this huge place where people buy and sell parts of companies, called stocks. But what does that really mean? Imagine if you and your friends wanted to start a lemonade stand, but you didn't have enough money to buy all the lemons, sugar, and cups. You might ask others to chip in some cash, and in return, those people own a tiny piece of your lemonade business. That's basically what happens when companies sell stocks. When you buy a stock, you own a small piece of that company.

Now, the stock market isn't just one building or a single website. It's actually a whole system full of marketplaces, like the New York Stock Exchange or the NASDAQ, where millions of people buy and sell stocks every day. Think of it like a giant online mall where people trade pieces of companies instead of clothes or gadgets. Prices of stocks can go up and down based on how well the company is doing, how investors feel about it, or even big events like new technology being invented or a company announcing a cool new product.

Why bother owning a piece of a company? Well, imagine if your lemonade stand becomes super popular and makes lots of money. If you own part of it, you get to share in those profits—that's called dividends. Also, if people think your lemonade stand is going to become the next big thing, the value of your piece can go up, so you could sell it later for more than you paid. That's how people make money investing in stocks: through dividends and selling stocks for a profit.

But the stock market isn't just about making quick cash. It's a place where your money can grow over time if you're patient. Not every stock will blow up overnight, but companies keep growing, inventing new stuff, or expanding their reach, which usually means the value of stocks rises slowly but steadily. That's why starting young can make a huge difference. Your investment has years to grow thanks to something called compound interest, but we'll dive into that more in another section.

It's normal to feel a little overwhelmed hearing about all this at first. The stock market might sound like a wild, fast-paced game where people with suits shout orders and millions of dollars change hands in seconds. Well, sometimes it can be like that, especially with day traders who buy and sell stocks super quickly. But for most people—especially starting out—the stock market is more like a long-term adventure. You pick stocks you believe in, hold on to them, and watch your investment grow over the years.

One cool thing about the stock market is that it's open to everyone. You don't need to be a billionaire or a Wall Street pro to buy stocks. Thanks to technology, teens can start investing with just a little bit of money through apps and platforms designed to be easy and safe. This accessibility means you can start learning how the market works by trying it yourself, building skills that will serve you well in the future.

Now, let's talk about what actually causes stock prices to move. Think about your favorite company—maybe one that makes video games, sneakers, or smartphones. If they announce a new product that sounds awesome, more people want to buy their stocks because they expect the company to make more money. This demand pushes the stock price up. On the flip side, if the company runs into trouble, like bad reviews, losing money, or legal issues, fewer people will want their stocks, so the price drops.

But there's more to it than just news about a company. Sometimes, the overall economy affects stock prices too. For example, if the economy is booming and people have more money to spend, many stocks tend to do well. If the economy starts to slow down, stock prices can fall because people get nervous about future profits. This is why you'll hear about "bull markets" (when prices are going up) and "bear markets" (when prices are going down). Just think of bulls charging ahead and bears retreating—they're symbols investors use to describe these trends.

It's important to know that stock prices don't always reflect the true value of a company. Sometimes they can be overhyped and get too expensive, or they might crash if investors panic. That's because the stock market doesn't just work on facts and numbers; emotions play a huge role. Fear and excitement can cause prices to swing wildly. This is exactly why investing requires patience and calm, especially at your age when you're just starting.

Here's an interesting fact: owning stocks means you might get to vote on certain company decisions. When companies have important votes, like choosing leaders or approving big plans, stockholders get a say based on how many shares they own. It's like being part of the company's team. This might not seem super exciting for a teen investor, but it's pretty cool knowing you have a voice—even if it's a small one.

Stock investing also comes with risks, and it's smart to understand them early on. Unlike putting money in a savings account where your cash is safe and slowly grows, stock prices can jump up and down fast. You could lose some or all of the money you invest if the company doesn't do well or if the market crashes. That's why people say "don't put all your eggs in one basket," meaning you should diversify your investments across many companies and industries to reduce risk.

The stock market also offers different types of stocks. For example, "growth stocks" belong to companies expected to grow quickly, like some tech startups. These can be exciting but sometimes riskier because the companies might not always succeed. Then there are "blue-chip stocks," which are shares in well-established companies known for steady earnings over time. These are usually safer but might not grow as fast. Choosing which type fits your goals and comfort with risk is part of becoming a smart investor.

Understanding the stock market doesn't mean you have to memorize complex charts or business jargon right away. Start simple: watch how companies you like perform in the market, follow news about new products or changes, and learn what makes investors excited or worried. Over time, you'll recognize patterns and develop your own investing style. Remember, every expert investor started where you are right now—curious and ready to learn.

One of the biggest advantages teens have is time. The longer you keep your money invested, the more opportunities your stocks have to grow, recover from dips, and benefit from compounding. This gives you a serious edge over people who wait until they're older to begin. Even if you start investing with just $50 or $100, those small amounts can add up over the years.

Also, don't let the stock market intimidate you. It's not about having secret formulas or insider info. It's about understanding companies you believe in, learning the basics, and making thoughtful decisions. It's perfectly okay to ask questions, make mistakes, and learn as you go. The important part is starting early and staying consistent.

Before jumping into buying stocks, take some time to practice with virtual stock market games or simulators. These let you trade fake money without risking real cash, so you can see how buying and selling stocks feels. Think of it like a flight simulator for pilots—it prepares you for the real thing while you're still learning.

In summary, the stock market is a place where people buy and sell tiny pieces of companies. Owning stocks means sharing in a company's success or failure. Prices move based on company performance, the economy, and investor emotions. While it comes with risks, it offers a powerful way to grow your money over time. Starting young gives you a huge advantage, and with patience, knowledge, and a smart approach, you can build real wealth. Remember, the stock market is not a magic box for fast cash but a tool for growing your financial future.

So the next time you hear about the stock market, don't think of it as some mystery meant only for adults. Think of it as an exciting opportunity for you to learn, grow, and take control of your money. You've got time, curiosity, and the ability to start building something amazing—one small stock at a time.

RISK VS. REWARD: HOW TEENS CAN PLAY IT SMART

When it comes to investing, the idea of risk can sound scary, especially if you're new to the game. But here's the kicker: risk isn't something to run away from—it's something to understand and manage. Every investment has some level of risk, but with risk also comes the potential for reward. Getting this balance right is one of the most important skills you can develop, whether you're 13 or 19. It's about knowing when to take chances, when to play it safe, and how to avoid common pitfalls that might cost you more than just money—it could cost your confidence and future opportunities.

Risk is basically the chance that you might lose some or all of the money you invest. On the flip side, reward means the potential to make money or grow your investment over time. Something that promises bigger rewards usually comes with bigger risks. So, if you want to make your money work hard for you, you need to figure out how much risk you're comfortable with and how much you want to aim for in return.

Think of investing like riding a bike. At first, it's tricky, and falling is part of the learning process. If you ride really fast (take high risks), you might get somewhere quicker, but you're also more likely to wipe out. Riding slower and steady (lower risk) means you might not cover as much ground right away, but you're less likely to fall and scrape your knees. Over time, learning how to find a middle ground that fits your style and goals is what lets you keep going and getting better.

One of the smartest things about being a teen investor is that you have a serious advantage: time. You can afford to take some calculated risks because you have years ahead to bounce back if things don't go as planned. This means you don't have to play it super safe at the start, but understanding your own limits is key. Don't just throw your money into something because it looks exciting or your friends say it's the next big thing. That's how you lose trust in yourself fast.

When teens ask, "How do I know if an investment is too risky?" the honest answer is—it depends. Your personal comfort zone, your goals, and how much you understand about where your money is going all matter. It's about being curious and asking questions before putting cash into anything. What are you investing in? How stable is it? What happens if things go south? Good investing means doing homework and not rushing.

Here's something that's often overlooked: playing it smart also means diversifying. Imagine not putting all your eggs in one basket, literally. Spreading your money across different investments reduces the chance that one bad choice ruins everything. Even with small amounts, you can mix things up between stocks, bonds, or funds, so when one investment dips, another might hold steady or even gain.

Now, not all risks are equal. There's a huge difference between gambling your allowance on a bet and thoughtfully investing part of your savings in a company you know and understand. Get clear on the difference between investing and speculating. The latter is more like a gamble—based on guesswork and hoping you get lucky—while investing is about learning, patience, and planning.

Sometimes the hardest part isn't the math or the markets—it's emotions. Fear and greed can trick even seasoned investors into making hasty decisions. Seeing the market drop might make you panic and sell right before the rebound, or hearing about a stock skyrocketing might tempt you to dive in without thinking. Learning to recognize those feelings and taking a step back before acting is a game changer.

Remember, playing it smart doesn't mean avoiding risks altogether. Like any challenge worth tackling, some risk is necessary for growth. Instead, think of it as taking informed risks. This means understanding the specific risks involved, the timeline you have, and your capacity to handle losses if they happen. For teens, this often means starting small, experimenting, and treating some investments as learning experiences.

Another big plus of investing as a teen is that you can afford to be patient. Investments need time to grow. If you're consistent and give your money enough time to compound and build, risks become less intimidating. This long view helps you weather the ups and downs instead of reacting to every blip or headline.

Getting familiar with risk also helps you make better choices about where to put your money first. Some investments, like government bonds or index funds, tend to carry lower risk but grow slower. On the other hand, individual stocks or emerging company shares can have higher ups and downs but might offer higher rewards if you pick carefully. Knowing this mix helps you build a strategy that suits your comfort and goals.

Playing it smart with risk also means setting a clear plan. Before investing, ask yourself specific questions: "What am I investing for?" "How soon will I need the money?" "What's the worst that could happen if this investment tanks?" When you have answers, you can make decisions that match your personal situation instead of following trends blindly.

Sometimes, playing it smart means saying no—or not yet. If an investment sounds too good to be true or you don't get how it works, hold off. Scams and risky schemes often prey on people excited about earning money fast, especially teens just starting out. Developing patience and a healthy skepticism will save you from bad decisions.

One more thing often missed: investing isn't just about money—it's about mindset. You're building a habit of weighing risks, making choices, and learning from your mistakes. These skills don't just help you with investing—they help you with every money move you'll make going forward.

So, how do you start playing it smart today? Begin by educating yourself. Read, watch, ask questions, and try paper trading (pretend investing) before committing real funds. Keep track of how different investments perform and how you feel about the ups and downs. With time, you'll become more comfortable with the risk-reward dance, and investing will feel less like a gamble and more like a tool you control to build the future you want.

Investing smart isn't about avoiding risk—it's about owning it. It's turning what seems like a scary challenge into a powerful opportunity. When you get this balance right, you're not just investing money—you're investing in yourself and your financial future.

CHAPTER 3

GETTING STARTED EVEN IF YOU HAVE $0

You might feel like diving into investing sounds impossible without money in your pocket, but the truth is, getting started doesn't require cash upfront—it starts with mindset and action. Before you see the first dollar grow, focus on opportunities to earn that first bit, whether it's odd jobs, freelancing your skills, or selling items you no longer need. It's about building habits that set you up for financial success and recognizing that every small step counts. You don't have to wait to be rich to start thinking like an investor; learning how to open an account (even if you're under 18), spotting good opportunities, and understanding simple tools can be done right now, no matter your balance. This chapter is about breaking down barriers and showing you that even with nothing, you can build a foundation that will turn into real wealth if you stick with it and stay curious.

HOW TO EARN YOUR FIRST $100 TO INVEST AS A TEEN

Starting with nothing can feel like a huge barrier, but making your first $100 as a teen isn't just possible—it can actually be pretty fun. Think of this as your launchpad toward building real wealth. The truth is, you don't need a fancy job or a trust fund to get going. What you do need is some creativity, determination, and a bit of hustle.

The world is full of opportunities if you know where to look. And even if you don't have access to traditional jobs, there are plenty of simple ways to begin earning money. The key is to start small. Whether it's helping neighbors, selling things you no longer need, or tapping into your talents, the goal is to get that first stack of cash rolling. Once you hit your first $100, you'll be surprised how much more motivated you become to keep going and grow your money.

The first step is to recognize what skills or resources you already have. Are you good at writing, graphic design, or social media? Can you tutor younger kids in math or help with tech? Maybe you're handy around the house and could offer lawn mowing or cleaning services. Even simple tasks like babysitting or dog walking can bring in consistent cash. These kinds of gigs don't require much upfront investment and can usually fit around your school schedule.

One of the easiest ways to start is by selling things you no longer use. Almost every teen has old clothes, video games, books, or gadgets lying around. Instead of letting them gather dust, put them up for sale online or at a local garage sale. Apps and websites like eBay, Depop, or Mercari make it simple to connect with buyers all over the country. Plus, you learn some valuable lessons about pricing, negotiation, and customer interaction. All those skills translate directly to managing money and investments later on.

Another overlooked way to earn money is by creating content. If you have any interest in video editing, photography, or blogging, consider building a small online presence. Platforms like TikTok, Instagram, or YouTube can become income sources once you grow your audience. Don't think you need millions of followers to get started—niche audiences are powerful, too. Sponsorship deals, affiliate marketing, and even direct selling become options the more you create and engage.

If online content isn't your thing, traditional side jobs still work wonders. Lawn care, snow shoveling, pet sitting, or running errands for busy neighbors can quickly add up. These jobs are flexible and let you control how many hours you work. Plus, they help develop a solid work ethic and responsibility, which are vital for long-term financial success. A simple flyer or a social media post in your neighborhood group can kick off these opportunities.

Don't underestimate the power of tutoring either. If you excel in a subject at school, many parents are on the lookout for help for their kids, especially in math, science, or languages. You can offer lessons either in person or virtually. The cool thing about tutoring is that it pays well compared to other teen jobs and also fixes your own knowledge deeper in your mind. Charging $15 to $25 an hour and tutoring for a few sessions each week could get you to that $100 milestone quickly.

One thing to watch out for is time management. Balancing school, extracurriculars, and your new money-making hustle can get overwhelming fast if you're not careful. Set aside specific hours each week dedicated solely to your side gig. Treat it like a mini business. This discipline not only helps you reach your $100 goal but also builds habits that will serve you in investing and beyond.

Another smart move is to think about skills you could quickly learn that have market value. Basic graphic design tools like Canva or Adobe Spark are user-friendly even for beginners, and lots of small businesses or local groups need help creating flyers, social media posts, or logos. Offering your services as a "designer in training" at a low rate can get you started and build a portfolio. You'll be surprised how many teens make a few hundred dollars just by helping local businesses with digital content.

If you've got more entrepreneurial spirit, consider offering something unique in your community. Think about what people might genuinely need. Could you run a car wash? Organize a neighborhood recycling program for cash? Host a weekend workshop teaching younger kids a skill you know? Being creative with your approach changes the game. This isn't just about making $100; it's about learning how to identify opportunities and take action without waiting for someone to hand you a paycheck.

When you start earning, keep track of all your income and expenses. It might sound boring, but this simple habit gives you a real snapshot of how your mini business is doing. You'll also feel more in control of your money, setting you up for smarter investing decisions down the road. Apps or even a notebook work great. Don't blow your earnings on impulse buys—try to set aside at least 80% of what you make for your investment fund. This connects the reward you worked hard to earn with your bigger money goals.

Finally, don't be afraid to ask for help or advice. Parents, teachers, or even friends with side hustles can offer helpful tips and motivation. There's no shame in starting small or not knowing exactly what to do right away. Every successful entrepreneur or investor began in a similar spot. The important part is you take the first step to earn that initial $100, because once you have it, your options for investing and growing your wealth truly open up.

Remember, this first $100 is more than just cash—it's a symbol of your self-reliance and potential. It represents your commitment to learning about money actively, not just passively hoping it will come to you. You're proving to yourself that you can earn, save, and take control of your financial future. That mindset will carry you far beyond this chapter and into the smart investments and wealth-building strategies that follow.

So look around, think creatively, and get ready to hustle. That first $100 is closer than you might think. It's waiting for you to grab it—and then put it to work building the future you want.

SETTING UP YOUR FIRST INVESTMENT ACCOUNT (YES, EVEN AS A MINOR)

So, you've learned the basics of money and investing, and you're ready to take the plunge by setting up your very first investment account. Here's the good news: you don't need to be an adult or even have a ton of cash saved up to get started. Even as a minor, you can open an investment account and start building your financial future. It might sound intimidating at first, but it's actually a lot simpler than most people think. Let's break down what you need to know to make this happen.

First off, understand that since you're under 18, you can't legally open a brokerage account on your own. The law requires someone older—a parent or guardian—to help you. This is called a "custodial account." Basically, an adult will set up the account in their name but for your benefit. While this might seem like a hurdle, it's actually a great way to learn alongside someone with more experience and build good financial habits together.

Custodial accounts come with different names depending on the financial institution, but the most common are called Uniform Gifts to Minors Act (UGMA) or Uniform Transfers to Minors Act (UTMA) accounts. Think of these as training wheels for investing. Your custodian manages the account until you turn 18 or 21 (depending on your state's rules), at which point full control passes to you. This gives you a safe environment to get familiar with the stock market without jumping into the deep end.

Choosing your custodian is important. Ideally, it should be someone you trust and who understands your financial goals. This isn't just about protection—it's also about mentorship. Having a parent or guardian who supports your investment journey means you can ask questions, share ideas, and get advice as you go. Plus, they'll help handle paperwork and verify your identity to open the account.

When it comes to picking the brokerage, look for platforms that are teen-friendly and don't require high minimum deposits. Several popular investment apps and firms now offer custodial accounts with no or low fees, making it easier to start small. You want a platform that's easy to navigate because the more comfortable you are with the tools, the more confident you'll feel placing your first trades. Some brokers even offer educational resources and gamified features to keep things interesting.

Another critical point: custodial accounts give you access to a wide range of investments. You can buy stocks, exchange-traded funds (ETFs), and even bonds once the money's in your account. Picking where to put your money comes next, but for now, focus on getting the account open and funded. Speaking of funding, the money deposited into custodial accounts becomes your property, even though you don't control the account yet. This is why it's important to treat investing seriously—because this is yours to grow over time.

Depositing money doesn't have to come from having a job already. You might get contributions from family gifts, birthday presents, or earnings from small gigs like lawn mowing, babysitting, or pet sitting. The key is to start small and be consistent. Even $10 or $20 can get things moving. Compound growth works best when you're regular about adding to your investment pot, so every little bit helps.

One more thing: setting up a custodial account means you're laying down a financial stepping stone that many adults wish they had started years ago. It's about creating a habit, understanding how investing works, and taking control of your financial future before you even reach legal adulthood. That early start gives you a massive advantage because time—your secret weapon—is on your side.

Now, you might wonder about taxes and legal rules tied to custodial accounts. While these can get a bit complex, the takeaway for now is this: any money you make in the account belongs to you and might be taxed under your name. However, the good news is that many teens fall under the threshold that requires them to pay taxes right away. Checking with a parent or guardian about specific tax situations helps, but don't let tax worries stop you from opening an account. Learning early about taxes is part of investing smart, but it's manageable once you start.

Also, security is a big deal. When setting up your account, make sure your custodian picks strong passwords and enables two-factor authentication if available. This protects your account from hackers and keeps your money safe while you focus on learning and growing your investments. In today's digital world, vigilance is part of being a smart investor.

After the account is set up and funded, the real adventure begins. Your first investment might be buying shares in a company you like or an ETF that tracks the market. But before you hit "buy," take some time to explore the tools your platform offers. Some have virtual trading accounts where you can practice without risking real money. Use those features to build confidence and test your strategies. Getting comfortable with the platform means you won't freeze up or make rushed decisions when it's time to invest real cash.

To sum it up, setting up your first investment account as a minor is absolutely doable, and honestly, it's one of the smartest money moves you can make as a teen. It requires teamwork, some paperwork, and a little patience, but the benefits are huge. You're setting yourself up for financial success and independence long before many adults even start thinking about investing.

Remember, the key isn't to make a fortune overnight, but to build a habit and grow your money step by step. With a custodian's support, a smart brokerage choice, and steady contributions—even if they're small—you'll be on your way to making the magic of investing work for you. This phase is about laying the foundation, so later on, when you're ready to manage your own account, you'll be ready to make wise decisions and own your financial future.

What to Look for in a Good Investment as a Beginner

So, you're ready to start investing—even if you don't have tons of cash lying around. That's awesome! But before you jump into investing your first dollar, it's important to know what makes a good investment, especially when you're new to the game. Picking the right investment isn't about guessing what will make you rich overnight. Instead, it's about understanding what you're putting your money into and making choices that help your money grow steadily over time.

One of the first things to look for in any investment is simplicity. When you're just getting started, the last thing you want is a confusing investment that requires a finance degree to understand. Good beginner investments are easy to grasp. For example, investing in low-cost index funds or exchange-traded funds (ETFs) is a smart move for many beginners because they spread your money across lots of companies instead of betting on just one. This way, you reduce risk—it's sort of like not putting all your eggs in one basket.

Speaking of risk, understanding how much risk you're willing to take is crucial. Everyone's risk tolerance is different, and as a beginner, you want to choose investments that won't keep you up at night. Generally, investments that promise super high returns quickly also come with higher risk, meaning you could lose your money. A good investment for a beginner balances risk and reward—offering growth potential without gambling your savings away. Think of it like riding a bike: you want to challenge yourself enough to get better, but not so much that you fall hard every time you try to pedal.

Another key factor is the cost of investing. Yes, some investments charge fees or commissions that can eat into your profits over time. This is often overlooked but super important. For beginners, keeping costs low means more of your money stays put to grow. Look for investments with low or no fees, especially on platforms designed for teens or beginners. High fees might seem small at first but could wipe out a huge chunk of your returns over the years.

Time is also on your side, especially as a teen. One of the best things about starting early is that even small amounts can grow significantly thanks to compound interest. This means the money you earn from investments starts making money on its own. So, when you choose an investment, think about how long you can leave your money there. Many good beginner options allow you to stay invested for the long haul without worrying about daily ups and downs. Remember, patience often pays off more than trying to "time the market" or hunt for quick wins.

It's also smart to look at the track record of the investment or the company behind it. While past performance doesn't guarantee the future, it gives you a snapshot of how consistent and stable an investment has been. If a company or fund has a history of steady growth over many years, that can be a good sign. Avoid investments that seem popular one day but crash or disappear the next. Stability matters, especially when you're just learning the ropes.

Transparency is another big deal. A good investment is one where you know exactly what's going on. You should be able to find clear, honest information about where your money is going, how it's being used, and what you can expect. Shady investments that don't explain these things should be avoided—if you can't understand it, it's probably not worth risking your hard-earned cash. Look for investments with plenty of information available and easy access to help if you have questions.

Diversification might sound like a fancy finance word, but it's super helpful. It just means spreading your money around rather than sticking it all in one place. A good investment strategy for beginners involves diversifying so that if one thing doesn't do well, your other investments can help balance the losses. Some beginner-friendly investments, like ETFs, do this automatically by including many different companies or industries in one package. Keep this in mind when you start building your portfolio—it's a simple way to lower risk right from the start.

Look for investments that match your personal interests or values, too. When you care about what you're investing in, it's easier to stay motivated. For example, some teens

64

choose companies focused on technology, green energy, or social causes. This connection can make the whole investing process more exciting and meaningful, keeping you curious and involved over time. Plus, it helps you learn more about industries you might want to work in or support later in life.

Flexibility is worth considering as well. Your financial goals and situation will change as you grow up. So, pick investments that let you adjust or add to your portfolio easily without high penalties or complicated rules. Some investment platforms made for teens and beginners are designed to be flexible, allowing you to start small, add money when you can, or even withdraw it if needed for emergencies. This flexibility can give you peace of mind while you're finding your footing in investing.

Don't forget about the educational aspect. Good beginner investments come with resources that help you learn along the way. Whether it's articles, videos, or tutorials, having access to clear explanations and tips can boost your confidence and help you make smarter choices. Many investment apps now include friendly, simple guides just for young investors, which makes the learning curve less intimidating.

Lastly, be cautious about investments that promise guaranteed huge returns or "get rich quick" schemes. These are often scams or extremely risky bets disguised as sure things. A smart beginner looks for realistic growth, not promises that sound too good to be true. Making money through investing takes time and patience, and sticking to trustworthy opportunities builds a solid foundation for your future wealth.

In short, a good investment for beginners is easy to understand, fits your risk level, charges low fees, and lets your money grow over time. It should be transparent, diversified, and flexible enough to match your changing goals. And most importantly, it's an opportunity for you to learn and grow financially. Starting with these types of investments doesn't just protect your money—it sets you up for success in building real wealth down the road.

You don't need to have a fortune to start investing wisely. With thoughtfulness, a little research, and patience, you can make choices that work for your current situation and your future dreams. Investing isn't just for adults or experts; it's for you. And by picking the right investments early on, you're already winning.

INVESTING APPS AND PLATFORMS PERFECT FOR TEENS

Starting to invest might seem like a big leap, especially if you're new to money management or have little cash to spare. Luckily, the rise of investing apps and platforms built with beginners in mind, including teens, is changing the game. These tools make investing accessible, easy to understand, and affordable. Whether you have $0 right now or just a small amount saved up, using the right app can set you on a real path toward growing your money and gaining confidence with investing.

First things first: many investing apps today don't have huge minimum deposit requirements—or any at all. This means you can dive in without needing a big chunk of cash upfront. Some platforms even let you buy fractional shares. This is a huge deal because instead of needing hundreds or thousands of dollars to buy a single share of a popular stock, you can invest just a few dollars or less. That way, you're not blocked out of the market just because your budget is tight. It's like being handed the keys to the investing world, even if your savings jar is barely half-full.

When you're looking for an app or platform, a few must-have features should be on your radar. Ease of use is key—if the app is confusing or has a steep learning curve, it's harder to stick with investing over time. Teens, in particular, need platforms that don't feel intimidating—think simple design and clear instructions. Educational resources built into these apps also help. You're not just throwing money into some mysterious market; you're learning what you own and why it matters. Many offer tutorials, explanations, and real-time tips that make investing less of a guessing game.

Another big plus is automatic investing or recurring deposits. Some platforms let you schedule small daily, weekly, or monthly investments straight from your bank account. This not only builds the habit of consistent investing but also takes advantage of dollar-cost averaging. That means you buy more shares when prices are low and fewer when prices are high, which helps smooth out market ups and downs in the long run. Consistency beats timing the market every time, especially when you're starting out.

Some investing platforms are specially designed for minors who might not be able to open accounts on their own. Custodial accounts, for example, let parents or guardians set up and manage accounts on behalf of their teens. These accounts are super helpful if you're under 18. They give you access to the stock market while still following legal guidelines, and once you turn 18 or 21 (depending on state laws), the account transfers to you fully. Look for apps that offer custodial accounts if you're not yet legally old enough to open an investment account solo.

Now, let's talk safety. Any investing app you pick should be regulated by official financial authorities. This protects your money and ensures the app follows important rules. Always double-check that your platform uses encryption to safeguard your personal information. Customer support availability is crucial, too. It's normal to have questions—especially in the beginning—so you want an app that provides clear, timely help when needed.

Another thing to consider is fees. Some apps advertise "zero commissions" on trades, meaning you don't get charged each time you buy or sell. But watch out for other hidden fees like account maintenance, inactivity fees, or withdrawal costs. Even small fees add up over time and can eat into your investment returns, especially when you're just starting with little money. Seek platforms with transparent fee structures—apps that show you exactly what you're paying upfront.

Your investment options matter too. While stocks get a lot of attention, some platforms open doors to other choices like exchange-traded funds (ETFs), bonds, or even cryptocurrencies. The more variety you have, the better you can learn what fits your goals and risk tolerance. However, beginners should steer clear of risky or complicated assets at first. Starting simple lets you build a strong foundation before moving into advanced strategies.

Here are a few standout apps and platforms popular with teens and first-time investors:

1. **Robinhood** is well-known for its easy-to-navigate app, no commission fees, and access to fractional shares. While it's aimed at a broad audience, younger investors often appreciate its clean design and straightforward approach. Just remember, this platform requires you to be 18 or older to open an account, so custodial setups are a must for younger teens.

2. **Acorns** is perfect if you want investing to happen without thinking much about it. It rounds up your everyday purchases to the nearest dollar and invests the spare change automatically. This "set it and forget it" style is ideal if you struggle to save consistently or feel overwhelmed. Plus, Acorns offers educational content to level up your financial knowledge.

3. **Stash** is another app designed with beginners in mind. It combines investing, banking, and budgeting tools all in one place—and it's super teen-friendly. Stash encourages small investments with educational tips sprinkled throughout the app, helping you understand why you're buying what you're buying.

4. **Stockpile** shines in its unique ability to offer gift cards that can be redeemed for stock. This means your family or friends can gift you shares instead of cash. It also offers fractional investing and custodial accounts, which makes it one of the most teen-accessible platforms out there.

5. **M1 Finance** is where you can get a bit more advanced with no trading fees and a focus on portfolio building. It encourages you to create "pies"—customized bundles of stocks and ETFs—and automatically balances them over time. That feature makes it easy to keep your investments diversified, even if you don't have a ton to start with.

Selecting the right app or platform isn't just about cool features; it's about picking something you'll actually use regularly. The best investing app for you is the one that fits your personality, age, lifestyle, and financial goals. If an app feels complicated, too expensive, or just plain boring, it's more likely you'll give up too soon. Remember, investing is a skill developed over time, and consistency trumps flashiness.

If your parents or guardians are involved—and they should be, especially for younger teens—use that as a chance to learn together. You can explore apps as a team, compare notes, and make decisions you all feel good about. A supportive investing environment can also keep you motivated. Plus, their experience might help you avoid beginner mistakes.

Once your account is set up and you've picked an app, start small. Even $5 invested now can grow substantially over time thanks to compound interest. The goal here isn't to become a millionaire overnight but to develop good habits that will pay off long after your teenage years. Buying your first fraction of a share can feel like winning a tiny battle — that momentum makes you want to keep going.

Keep in mind that technology keeps evolving. New apps and platforms pop up all the time with fresh features and better options. Make it a habit to stay informed. Join communities where young investors trade tips, subscribe to newsletters, or follow financial blogs aimed at teens. Your future self will thank you for staying curious and open.

In the end, investing apps and platforms aren't just tools; they're bridges to financial independence. They turn complicated money topics into manageable steps and encourage progress, even if your bank account is nearly empty. You don't need to wait for "the right time" or "a pile of cash" to begin building wealth. The digital age has dropped powerful investing opportunities right into your pocket—now it's your move.

STEP-BY-STEP: MAKING YOUR FIRST INVESTMENT

So, now that you've earned some money and set up your first investment account, it's time to take the next big step—actually making your first investment. This might feel a little scary at first, and that's completely normal. After all, you're about to put your hard-earned money to work. But trust me, there's no secret formula, and you don't need to be rich or have a finance degree. Investing is simply about making smart moves, one step at a time.

Let's break it down. First, you have to decide what you want to invest in. Remember from earlier sections, investments can be stocks, ETFs, bonds, or even a small business venture. For your first go, it's best to start simple—a low-cost exchange-traded fund (ETF) or fractional shares of a popular company often make great entry points. These options spread risk across many companies or let you buy a tiny piece of big companies, making it easier and safer for beginners.

Before you buy anything, do a quick review of your finances. It's tempting to throw all your money into one stock you heard about. But instead, ask yourself, "How much can I comfortably invest without needing this money soon?" Your emergency savings and everyday budget should stay untouched. Your investment money is ideally what you won't need for a while—years, even—so it has time to grow.

Once you've chosen what to invest in and set your budget, it's time to open your investment app or platform. Most apps designed for teens are super user-friendly, guiding you step-by-step through the process. You'll usually start by searching for the ticker symbol of the stock or ETF. If you don't know the ticker, a quick Google search like "Apple stock ticker" or "S&P 500 ETF ticker" will get you the info.

After finding your investment, select "Buy." Here's where things get interesting. You'll have the option to specify how many shares or fractional shares you want to buy. Fractional shares let you buy less than a full share, which is perfect when prices are high. For example, if one share of a company costs $500, you can still invest $50 and own 0.1 shares. Enter the amount you want to invest based on your budget and confirm the order. Most apps will show you an estimated fee before finalizing the purchase. Fees might be tiny or even zero, depending on the platform—always double-check to avoid surprises.

What happens next is kind of like magic but based on simple rules. Your money is converted into ownership of a piece of that company or fund. You'll see your investment on your app's dashboard, and just like that, you've officially joined the investing club! Don't get discouraged if the value goes up and down at first. It's completely normal, especially in your early days.

One thing many beginners overlook is tracking their investment's performance without obsessing over daily price swings. Imagine checking your stock every five minutes—it can stress you out and tempt you to make rash decisions. Instead, set a schedule to review your portfolio weekly or monthly. This helps you stay informed while keeping your cool.

Another smart move when making your first investment is to think long term. Investing isn't about getting rich overnight. It's about growing your money steadily over years. The more patient you are, the more powerful compound interest becomes. Your investment's profits can start earning their own profits—that's a game changer. So, rather than focusing on quick wins, aim for steady progress, and you'll build confidence along the way.

Now, let's talk about mistakes because they're going to happen, and that's okay. Maybe you pick a stock that doesn't perform well or invest at the wrong time. It's all part of learning. The key is not to panic and not to throw in the towel. When you mess up, analyze what happened, adjust your strategy, and keep going. Every investor, even the big-time pros, has faced losses. The difference is they learn and take their lessons into the next move.

Also, don't feel pressure to invest a huge amount all at once. In fact, making smaller investments over time is often smarter. This approach is called dollar-cost averaging. By investing a fixed amount regularly—say $20 every week or month—you buy more shares when prices are low and fewer when prices are high. Over time, this smooths out the price you pay and lowers the risk of investing everything at the wrong moment.

When you place your first order successfully, celebrate that win! Getting started is the hardest part for many people. You just took control of your financial future, which is huge. But remember, investing isn't a "set it and forget it" game either. You'll want to keep learning and adjusting your strategy as you gain experience. Over time, consider diversifying your investments instead of putting all your money in one spot. A balanced portfolio protects you from the ups and downs of individual stocks.

One last thing: always keep your goals in mind. Did you start investing to buy a car in a few years? To save for college? Or just to see how this whole investing thing works? Knowing your why helps prevent impulsive decisions driven by hype or fear. It also keeps you motivated to stay consistent, even when the market zigzags.

In summary, here's your simple checklist to making your first investment:

1. Decide what type of investment suits you (start with ETFs or fractional shares).
2. Set aside money you won't need immediately.
3. Open your investing app and find your chosen investment by ticker symbol.
4. Enter the amount to invest and confirm the purchase.

5. Track your investment regularly but avoid obsessing over daily changes.

6. Practice patience and focus on long-term growth.

7. Learn from mistakes and keep investing steadily with dollar-cost averaging.

Making your first investment is more than just buying stocks. It's about starting a journey towards financial independence and building habits that last a lifetime. Each step you take now adds up to a future where money works for you instead of the other way around. So, take that first step confidently—you're already ahead of most people your age who wait too long to start.

CHAPTER 4

MINDSET, HABITS & REAL-LIFE SKILLS FOR WEALTH

Building wealth isn't just about knowing how to invest or save; it starts with the right mindset and habits that stick with you long term. When you think like an investor instead of a spender, every dollar becomes a tool to grow your future, not just something to blow on instant gratification. Real-life skills like spotting scams, ignoring hype from social media "experts," and staying consistent with your goals—even when your friends don't get it—are the secret sauce to lasting success. Developing good habits early, like tracking your money, seeking smart side hustles, and learning from mistakes, gives you a huge advantage. The difference between teens who just dream about being millionaires and those who actually become them lies in everyday choices and persistence, not luck. It's about setting yourself up with habits and attitudes that help you keep moving forward no matter what.

Think Like an Investor, Not a Spender

When you start thinking about money, it's easy to get caught up in what you can buy right now. New sneakers, the latest phone, or even just grabbing food with friends often seems like the most exciting way to spend your cash. But shifting your mindset from a spender to an investor sets the groundwork for building wealth that lasts. Instead of asking how fast you can spend your money, start asking how you can make that money work for you. This mental switch might seem small, but it changes everything.

Investing is about planting seeds for the future. Imagine you have $20—you could spend it on something fun today, or you could invest it in something that might grow to be $100 someday. Which sounds better? The idea isn't just about saving, because saving is sitting on money. Investing means putting your money into things that have the potential to grow in value over time. It's about patience, smart decisions, and understanding that wealth doesn't appear overnight.

Most people think investing is only for the wealthy, or people way older than you. But that's a myth. The reality is that starting young gives you a huge advantage. The longer your money stays invested, the more it can grow thanks to compound interest—the magic of earning money on money. So thinking like an investor means putting your future self first, even if it means saying no to some stuff you really want today.

But how do you get into an investor's mindset instead of a spender's? First, focus on goals that go beyond instant gratification. Maybe you want to save for college, buy your first car, or even open a small business one day. When you make spending decisions, ask yourself: does this help me reach those goals? If the answer isn't yes, it might be worth reconsidering.

Another big part of thinking like an investor is learning to delay gratification. That means resisting the urge to spend money as soon as you get it. It's tough, especially since we live in a world full of temptations and ads everywhere telling you to buy now. But think about it this way: every dollar you don't spend today can be an extra dollar that grows into many more dollars in the future.

It's also important to realize that spending and investing aren't enemies. The key is balance. You still need to enjoy life and treat yourself, but not at the expense of your financial future. Developing this balance is a habit. The sooner you practice it, the easier it becomes. Imagine how proud you'll feel in a few years when your money has grown because you made smart choices early on.

When you think like an investor, you start paying attention to money differently. You notice where your cash goes, and you watch out for impulsive buys that don't add value. Instead, you look for opportunities where spending money could actually be a smart investment. This might be buying books that teach new skills, taking online courses that increase your earning potential, or even investing in yourself through sports or arts that build confidence and discipline. These kinds of "investments" pay off in ways money alone can't buy.

Most adults who are financially successful didn't get there by luck. They developed habits over time, like prioritizing investing, learning about money, and thinking ahead. The mindset they have is what sets them apart from people who just spend everything they earn. This mindset also helps them weather tough times, like when the market dips or unexpected expenses pop up. Instead of freaking out and selling everything, they stay calm and keep focused on long-term goals.

Another difference between a spender and an investor is how they see risk. Spenders rarely think about risk because they're focused on the next purchase. Investors see risk as something to manage carefully. They understand that all investments come with ups and downs, but they also believe that with patience and knowledge, those risks can be minimized. Learning about risk early helps you avoid bad decisions, like falling for "get rich quick" schemes or spending impulsively to keep up with others.

How do you start building this mindset today? Start by tracking your spending for a week. Write down everything— yes, even the small things like a soda or a candy bar. Seeing where your money goes lets you decide what to cut back on if you want to invest more. Next, set a tiny investment goal. It could be putting $5 a week into a savings or investment account. The amount doesn't matter as much as building the habit of choosing investing over spending.

Remember, thinking like an investor doesn't mean being perfect. It means being intentional about your money. You won't get it right all the time, and that's okay. Even the best investors make mistakes. What matters is learning from those mistakes and adjusting your habits.

There's also a sense of freedom that comes with an investor's mindset. When your money grows, you're not tied to needing a job just to pay bills. You create options for yourself. Whether it's paying for college without loans, traveling, or starting a business, your money gives you choices. That's powerful—way more powerful than any toy or gadget you could buy today.

Surround yourself with people who think the same way. It's easier to make smart financial choices if your friends support your goals instead of pressuring you to spend. Talk about investing with family or teachers who understand finance. The more you practice the investor mindset, the more natural it will feel.

In the end, thinking like an investor is about respect for your future. It's about caring enough to make decisions that might not be fun right now but will pay off big later. Spending money feels good in the moment, but investing money creates possibilities that last forever. So next time you get some cash, pause and ask yourself: am I spending or investing? Your answer just might change your life.

Avoiding Scams, FOMO, and TikTok "Gurus"

Jumping into the world of investing and wealth-building can feel exciting. It's easy to get swept up in the hype when you see someone on TikTok promising quick riches or hear about a "can't-miss" opportunity from a friend. But here's the reality: not everything that glitters online is gold. In fact, a ton of what gets shared on social media about investing is either misleading or downright dangerous. Learning to spot scams, resist FOMO (fear of missing out), and ignore so-called "gurus" is an essential skill. It protects your money, your time, and your confidence.

Scams often prey on the excitement and enthusiasm that teens bring to investing. Someone might promise a "guaranteed 100% return" or say you can "get rich overnight" by following their advice. These claims should immediately raise red flags. The truth is, no one can promise a sure thing, especially in investing. The markets go up and down. Building wealth takes time, patience, and smart decisions—not magic tricks or secret tips.

Social media plays a big role in how teens learn about money today, but it can be a double-edged sword. TikTok, Instagram, and similar platforms are packed with creators sharing everything from investing tips to motivational talks. While some of this content is helpful, a lot is just for views and likes. People may exaggerate their success or offer strategies that are straight-up risky. Sometimes they're even trying to sell you products, courses, or memberships that don't add real value. When you scroll through your feed, it's critical to approach what you see with a healthy dose of skepticism.

One of the biggest traps leading teens astray is FOMO—fear of missing out. This feeling shoots up when you see others talking about the latest "hot stock," crypto coin, or side hustle. Suddenly, it feels like if you don't jump in right now, you'll be left behind forever. The problem is, FOMO tends to push people into impulsive moves. Instead of thinking through whether an investment fits your goals or risk level, you buy because everyone else is. That's a recipe for stress and often, losses.

Remember, nobody needs to chase every trend. Wealth isn't built on last-minute grabs or timing the market perfectly. It grows steadily through consistent habits and wise choices. When FOMO kicks in, pause and ask yourself if this investment or "opportunity" matches what you've learned about your own financial goals, your comfort level with risk, and your timeline. If the answer isn't a clear yes, it's usually best to step back.

Then there are the TikTok "gurus." The label "guru" might make someone sound like an expert or financial genius, but don't be fooled by snappy editing, slick production, or even a huge following. Some of these people have little real experience, and many make their money not from investing but from selling advice, merch, or courses. Before taking advice seriously, ask yourself: What are their credentials? Can they show a long history of successful investing? Are they transparent about risks and losses, or do they only talk about wins?

Another key point is that financial advice is rarely one-size-fits-all. What works for a 30-year-old with a full-time salary might not make sense for a teenager just starting out. Most so-called gurus offer vague strategies designed to appeal to everyone, but building wealth takes personal planning and understanding your own financial situation. Always seek information from multiple trustworthy sources before making decisions. Books, reputable websites, and guidance from real financial advisors are much safer bets than flashy social media personalities.

Let's talk about how to protect yourself. First, never give out your personal or financial information to strangers online. Scammers often try to lure you into sharing passwords, banking details, or social security numbers. A solid rule is to never trust unsolicited requests and always verify through official channels.

Second, be wary of any investment opportunity that demands quick action or rushing your decision. Phrases like "act now," "limited spots," or "guaranteed profits" are classic signs of pressure tactics. Take your time. Research the investment, read reviews, and ask questions. If something smells fishy, it probably is.

It's also smart to develop critical thinking skills around financial content. When you watch a video about a hot stock tip, try to analyze the reasoning behind it rather than just the hype. What's the company's business model? Are there risks

84

mentioned? Do they explain why the stock might go up or is this just a flashy headline? Learning to ask these questions early will help you sift through noise and focus on what truly matters.

One mistake many teens make is confusing investing with gambling. Buying stocks based on tips from random internet strangers or jumping into volatile cryptocurrencies without understanding them is more like playing the lottery. Investing is about research, patience, and long-term growth. It's about making smart bets on companies you believe will be successful over years, not trying to win a quick jackpot.

Part of avoiding scams and FOMO is knowing your own financial plan well enough to say "no" confidently. When you set clear goals and understand why you're investing, it's easier to tune out distractions. For example, if your plan is to build a diversified portfolio with steady growth over five years, a flashy meme stock or pump-and-dump scheme probably doesn't fit. Sticking to your strategy protects your money and keeps you focused on the bigger prize.

Another useful habit is sharing your thoughts or questions with someone you trust—maybe a parent, teacher, or a knowledgeable friend. When you run ideas by others, you get another perspective and reduce the chances of falling for slick sales pitches or scams. Plus, talking openly about your investing journey helps you learn faster and builds confidence.

Remember, the goal isn't to avoid risk completely—investing always involves some—but to take smart, informed

85

risks that increase your chances of success. Scams, hype, and get-rich-quick schemes get you nowhere because they're based on fooling you, not offering real value. Developing a mindset that values education, patience, and sensible decision-making is the best defense you have.

In the bigger picture, avoiding scams and FOMO is about protecting your future self. It might seem tempting to chase after the latest shiny thing, but building wealth is about putting your resources on a solid foundation. Think of your money as seeds for a garden. You want to plant them carefully, nurture them over time, and resist shaking the soil every time a new "shiny object" appears.

Starting young gives you a massive advantage. You have time on your side to learn, make mistakes, and recover. Don't waste that by rushing into things you don't understand or following strangers who promise easy wins. Instead, focus on building solid financial habits, staying curious, and asking critical questions. That's how you'll grow real confidence and real wealth over time.

In the end, your best investment isn't a stock or crypto—it's your ability to recognize what's real, what's risky, and what's just hype. Developing that skill now will serve you well throughout your life, helping you make smart decisions not only with money but with any big choice you face. Stay sharp, stay patient, and keep your eyes open. Your financial future depends on it.

HOW TO STAY CONSISTENT WHEN FRIENDS DON'T GET IT

When you start thinking seriously about money, investing, and building wealth, it's pretty common for your friends to not totally understand what you're doing— or why you're doing it. Maybe they're more interested in spending their cash on the latest kicks or the newest games, while you're focused on saving up or learning how to invest your first hundred bucks. That difference can feel weird or even isolating. It's tough to stay consistent when the people around you don't share your mindset or priorities.

But here's the truth: Developing good financial habits early is one of the smartest moves you can make, even if it means swimming against the current. At this point in your life, the choices you make build the foundation of your financial future. So, when your friends don't get it, don't let that stop you. In fact, learn to use that as fuel to keep going stronger.

One thing you can remind yourself is that you're not doing this to impress anyone right now. Building wealth and mastering money is a long game. The benefits won't always be obvious or exciting in the moment—and that's okay. Your friends are in a different place with their money mindset, but that doesn't mean yours is wrong. Everyone's journey is unique, and you're setting yourself up to win in the long run.

When you explain your goals or habits to friends and they don't really get it, try not to get frustrated. Instead, think of it as practice for communicating and owning your decisions. You don't need to convince them to change their ways, but being clear on why you're making certain choices helps reinforce your own commitment. Sometimes just saying it out loud, whether to friends or yourself, cements your resolve.

Consistency really comes down to focus and routine. If you've committed to saving a certain amount every week or researching an investment opportunity regularly, treating it like a habit rather than a chore can make a huge difference. Habits aren't about motivation alone—they're about building a system that you can rely on even when you don't feel particularly inspired. And when friends invite you to blow your cash or skip saving, your habits serve as your personal guardrails.

Another thing to keep in mind is that peer pressure can come in subtle forms. It's not always a direct "Why are you so boring with your money?" Sometimes it's simply the vibe of hanging out in ways that drain your budget or distract you from your goals. Learning how to say no or set boundaries without feeling awkward is a skill you develop over time. You'll find that friends respect you more when you stand firm, and some might even start to think differently about their own money in response.

It helps to find your motivation in your vision of the future rather than the opinions of people around you. Picture what financial freedom looks like for you—a future where you don't have to stress about bills, where you can choose a career you love without worrying about money, or even take time off to travel or pursue passions. That vision is powerful fuel when the present moment feels tough or lonely.

At the same time, don't be afraid to seek out like-minded people. There are tons of teens who are just as curious and focused on building wealth as you are. It might take a bit of searching—online communities, investment clubs, or even groups at school—but connecting with others who share your goals can be hugely motivating. They'll push you to keep going when your usual circle doesn't. Surrounding yourself with people who "get it" helps normalize the habits you're building and makes the process more fun.

Make space for celebrating even the small wins along your journey. Did you save your first $50? Made your first investment? Avoided a purchase you didn't need? Those moments matter. Acknowledging progress, no matter how small, builds confidence and momentum. It also reminds you that what you're doing is worthwhile, even if your friends don't fully understand it yet.

Also, remember that your relationship with money doesn't have to be lonely. Share your knowledge in light doses and in positive ways. You might find that when you talk about investing or saving not with judgment but with curiosity and excitement, some friends will start to listen. Maybe they won't jump on board immediately, but planting seeds of financial literacy always has value. You could be changing someone's money mindset without even realizing it.

There will be times when your friends' attitudes toward money clash with yours. Maybe they see you as "too serious" or "boring" because you pass up spending on parties, fast food, or the newest gadgets. Those moments sting, but they're part of growing up and figuring out who you are. It's natural to want acceptance, but know that staying true to your financial goals means prioritizing your future self over short-term approval from others.

Treat negative or skeptical comments as an opportunity to practice resilience. Instead of reacting emotionally, you can keep your response simple and firm. Something like, "Yeah, I'm saving for something important right now," or "I have different priorities with my money" works fine. You don't owe anyone a big explanation. Your consistency is your answer.

It's also useful to remind yourself why you started and who you're doing this for. Sometimes when friends don't get it, you might question your own commitment. That's normal. But come back to the reasons that motivate you—whether it's supporting your family someday, creating financial independence, or even just proving to yourself that you can do it. Those reasons help rebuild your enthusiasm every time.

Consistency becomes easier when you track your progress then reflect on it regularly. Keep a journal, a spreadsheet, or use an app to log your savings or investment milestones. When you see your progress visually, it's harder to doubt your path or feel distracted by what others are doing.

Plus, it turns saving and investing into a game where you're leveling up your financial skills instead of just denying yourself fun.

One more thing: learning to manage your emotions around money is a crucial part of staying consistent. It's easy to get discouraged when you see others spending freely or when your investments don't grow as quickly as you hoped. But patience and emotional control go hand-in-hand with financial success. Stick to your habits even when the rewards aren't immediate, because the real magic of building wealth happens over time.

In the end, the people around you might not always understand your money mindset, but your future self will thank you every step of the way. Staying consistent isn't about being perfect; it's about showing up for yourself, day after day, investing in your dreams even when it's tough. Your financial habits, your discipline, and your focus will shape a future where you get to call the shots.

So keep going. Build the habits that matter. Stay focused on your vision. And remember, you're setting a powerful example—even if your friends don't get it right now.

SIDE HUSTLES FOR TEENS TO BOOST INVESTING POWER

One of the fastest ways for teens to take control of their financial future is by starting a side hustle. You've probably heard the term tossed around a lot, but what it really means is a way to earn money outside of your regular school or home responsibilities. The beauty of side hustles is that they don't just bring in cash—they build essential habits like discipline, creativity, and independence. All of these eventually boost your investing power by giving you more money to put toward your future rather than spending it all on instant gratification.

Think about it: starting a small gig or project that makes money gives you an edge. Instead of waiting around for a birthday gift or allowance, you're creating your own opportunities to grow your bank account. This isn't just about earning; it's the foundation for developing an investor's mindset. When you hustle, you learn how to weigh risks and rewards on a real level. For instance, deciding how much time to invest in your side gig versus how much cash you want to save or invest involves choices—just like picking stocks.

Now, you don't need to launch a full-blown business to start hustling. Some side hustles are low-key yet effective. Babysitting, dog walking, tutoring, lawn care, or even selling handmade crafts online can quickly turn pocket change into serious investing money. The key is consistency and treating it like a real job, no matter how small it seems. Real wealth builds from real effort.

But side hustles aren't just about the money coming in. They teach you time management and problem-solving, skills investors swear by. For example, handling clients, juggling school projects, and your side income all at once builds a sense of responsibility that transfers directly to managing your portfolio.

Being a teen with a side hustle also means understanding the value of every dollar earned. You start to think differently about cash when it's your blood, sweat, and tears behind it. Instead of mindlessly spending, you're more likely to set specific goals: save a portion, reinvest a portion, and maybe reward yourself. This kind of financial discipline is pure gold when it comes to investing.

Some teen side hustlers go beyond traditional hustles and dive into digital gigs. Social media skills, graphic design, content creation, or coding bring high demand for freelance teen workers today. Not only do these skills pay well, but they're highly portable—meaning you can do them from anywhere. This flexibility helps you keep focus on your investing journey without burning out from too many commitments.

Another advantage of starting young is the power of compounding knowledge. The earlier you begin, the more you learn about what works and what doesn't in the real financial world. Side hustles often force quick problem-solving: What should I charge? How do I market myself? How do I handle taxes? These pressing questions nudge you to build financial literacy the practical way, fast-tracking your growth as a teen investor.

Maybe the biggest motivator for teen side hustlers is the exciting sense of ownership. You're not just waiting for money to come to you; you're making it happen. This proactive approach feels empowering and makes the idea of investing less intimidating. When you've earned your money, you become more curious about multiplying it through investments rather than just watching it sit in a savings account.

Starting a side hustle isn't always smooth sailing, though. You might face setbacks—like clients backing out, fluctuating demand, or balancing school with work. What matters most is how you handle these obstacles. Those who keep pushing through develop resilience, a vital trait for any investor. The markets will have ups and downs, but a side hustle teaches you early how to weather uncertainty and keep moving forward.

Getting started can seem scary if you haven't tried it before. But the good news is many teens already have skills or hobbies that can turn into income streams. Are you good at writing or editing? Consider freelance gigs. Do you have a knack for photography or creating videos? Social media and local events always need fresh content. Even being a connector—someone who links buyers to sellers—can be a hustle.

A side hustle can fit around your unique schedule and interests, which means it's not a one-size-fits-all deal. Some teens prefer side projects that don't require constant contact, like selling products online, while others thrive on interactive hustles like tutoring or coaching sports. Explore whatever feels natural; the best side hustle is the one you'll stick with.

As your side hustle grows, think about scaling it. Could you outsource parts of the work? Or reinvest your earnings into tools that increase your efficiency? Scaling doesn't have to wait until you're an adult—these early lessons are perfect low-risk experiments in entrepreneurship and money management.

Most importantly, track every dollar you earn from your side hustle separately from your allowance or other income. When you see how your hustle grows, it'll motivate you to allocate part of that money directly into investments. This habit makes investing a natural extension of your money mindset, not something abstract or "too complicated" for teens.

Let's face it, investing with nothing saved isn't possible, so the faster you build up your capital, the better the investing opportunities you'll encounter. Even making an extra $50 a month adds up over time, especially if you put it straight into investments that earn returns. That's the real power behind side hustles—they create the fuel for your investing engine.

Finally, keep in mind the importance of balance. Your side hustle should enhance your life, not stress you out or pull you away from your bigger goals. Setting boundaries around time and energy is just as important as earning money. Learning to say no is a skill that protects your focus—both for your hustle and your investing journey.

To sum it up, side hustles are more than just a way to make cash. They're practice in financial independence, focus, and goal-setting. Starting one today doesn't just build your wallet; it trains your mind to think like an investor ready to grab opportunities and handle challenges. Every dollar earned carries the potential to grow, but even more valuable is the growth you experience in managing your hustle. That's how teens truly boost their investing power.

WHAT MILLIONAIRE TEENS DO DIFFERENTLY

When you think about millionaire teens, it's easy to assume they're just lucky or born into money. But that's rarely the case. What sets these teens apart isn't just the cash flow—it's their mindset, habits, and the way they approach real-life money skills. They think differently about wealth, and they act differently around it. Understanding these differences can make a huge impact on how you build your own financial future.

First, millionaire teens are intentional with their time and energy. They don't just follow the crowd or chase the latest trends without purpose. Instead, they focus on learning and practicing skills that help them grow wealth over the long haul. This means dedicating time to understanding investments, tracking their spending, or building side hustles that create real income. They don't wait for opportunities to drop from the sky—they make opportunities themselves.

Another big difference lies in their attitude toward money and risk. While many teens might shy away from investing because it feels risky or confusing, millionaire teens see risk as just part of the game. They don't recklessly throw money into something without homework, but they embrace calculated risks. They know that avoiding risks altogether often leads to missed chances. That willingness to step out of their comfort zone with a clear plan is a defining habit.

Speaking of plans, millionaire teens don't just rely on goals that sound good—they make SMART goals: Specific, Measurable, Achievable, Relevant, and Time-bound. Their goals aren't vague hopes like "I want to be rich someday." Instead, it's things like "I want to save $1,000 by the end of the school year" or "I'm going to invest $50 every month starting now." These clear targets act as a roadmap and keep them accountable.

One thing you'll notice is how millionaire teens treat money like a tool—not just a reward. They get that money isn't just for spending on fun stuff, but it's what opens doors to bigger opportunities. They're constantly thinking about how each dollar can work harder for them, whether that means saving, investing, or reinvesting earnings back into their ventures. The key is mindset: money's purpose is to build wealth, not just to burn through quickly.

Millionaire teens are also really consistent. It's easy to get excited about making some cash or scoring a first investment, but it takes discipline to stick with it over months and years. These teens show up every day, manage their investments regularly, track their progress, and make adjustments instead of giving up when things don't turn out perfectly fast. They understand that real wealth doesn't explode overnight—it's the result of steady progress and persistence.

Another habit that separates millionaire teens is how they seek knowledge. They don't rely solely on what they pick up in school or from mainstream media. Instead, they actively look for out-of-the-box resources like books, podcasts, blogs, and mentors to deepen their financial understanding. They know the more they learn, the better decisions they can make. This hunger for knowledge is a powerful driver that keeps improving their approach and expanding their horizons.

Many millionaire teens also recognize the power of networking. They surround themselves with like-minded peers and adults who encourage their growth. Instead of stepping on others to get ahead, they build genuine relationships that open doors and create win-win situations. Whether it's finding partners for side hustles, getting advice from experienced investors, or simply motivating each other, this network acts like a support system that fuels their success.

Importantly, millionaire teens avoid giving in to FOMO—fear of missing out—especially around flashy purchases or risky "get rich quick" schemes often hyped online. They've learned to filter out noise and focus on what truly matters. This helps them stay away from scams, impulsive decisions, and distractions that eat away at their financial goals. Instead of following every trend, they rely on research and patience.

Millionaire teens also know how to manage emotions when it comes to money. Money can stir up feelings like excitement, fear, or envy, and those emotions can cloud judgment if you're not careful. They practice staying rational and focused, especially when markets fluctuate or when friends tease them for being careful. Controlling emotions means they avoid impulsive buys, panic selling, or burnout from trying to do too much too fast.

Another crucial thing millionaire teens do differently is they learn from failures instead of fearing them. Nobody's perfect, and setbacks happen. But these teens use mistakes as valuable lessons. If an investment doesn't perform well, or a side hustle hits a rough patch, they reflect on what went wrong and adjust their game plan. Rather than giving up, they bounce back smarter and more prepared.

One of the biggest differences is how millionaire teens value their own time and skills. They understand that their greatest asset is their ability to learn and create, not just the money they have right now. This means they invest in themselves by building skills that pay off in the long term— things like communication, problem-solving, creativity, and financial literacy. These aren't just school skills; they're life skills that multiply their earning potential over time.

Millionaire teens are also proactive about creating multiple income streams. They don't rely on a single source like allowances or one job. Instead, they build side hustles, invest in stocks or crypto, create digital content, or even start small businesses. This diversity reduces their risk and accelerates wealth-building. They know that when one avenue slows down, others keep working.

Finally, millionaire teens think big but start small. They set ambitious dreams—like owning properties, funding college without loans, or launching their own companies— but they begin with manageable steps. They don't wait to be experts or have thousands of dollars. They experiment with what they have and grow from there. This combination of big-picture vision and practical action is what moves them forward every day.

Understanding these key differences isn't just inspiring; it's actionable. The habits and mindset of millionaire teens are things you can adopt starting today. It's about making conscious choices, being curious, and staying disciplined. Wealth-building isn't a secret club—it's a skill set that anyone willing to learn and practice can master.

CHAPTER 5

YOUR WEALTH-BUILDING ROADMAP

Now that you've got the basics and mindset settled, it's time to map out a clear plan that guides your money moves from today into the future. Building wealth isn't about luck or secret tricks—it's about creating a strategy that grows with you as your knowledge, income, and goals evolve. Think of this roadmap as your personal GPS, helping you decide when to save, invest, and even take smart risks without losing sight of your long-term vision. By setting milestones and adjusting to life's twists, you'll stay on track even when markets fluctuate or distractions pop up. Remember, wealth-building is a journey that anyone can start early, and the sooner you set your path, the more time your money has to work for you. This chapter lays out how to build that adaptable, confident approach that keeps your financial future bright and flexible.

How to Build a Portfolio That Grows with You

Building a portfolio isn't just about throwing money at stocks or investments and hoping they grow. It's a bit like planting a garden—you want to choose the right seeds, take care of them, and watch them develop over time. And most importantly, your portfolio should evolve as you do. Because the person you are at 15 is not the same person you'll be at 25 or 30, your investments should adapt along the way.

Let's start by understanding what it means to have a portfolio that "grows with you." In simple terms, it means your investments change as your goals, income, and risk tolerance change. When you're a teenager, for example, you might be able to take bigger risks because you have plenty of time to recover from losses. But as you get older and start saving for things like college, a car, or a first apartment, you might want to shift towards safer investments. Your portfolio reflects these shifting priorities.

One of the first things to keep in mind is balance. Think of a portfolio like a music playlist. You want a good mix of songs—some fast and high-energy, others slow and relaxing. In investing, the "songs" are different types of assets like stocks, bonds, and cash. Stocks usually offer higher growth but with higher ups and downs. Bonds tend to be more stable but with lower returns. Cash might not grow much but gives you safety and quick access to money when you need it. Having a well-balanced portfolio helps you ride out the rough patches without losing your cool.

Don't fall into the trap of putting all your money into just one stock or one company because it's "cool" or because your favorite YouTuber talked about it. That's called putting all your eggs in one basket. What if that basket drops? So instead, spread your investments across different areas. This is called diversification, and it's a strategy that helps protect your money. You might invest in tech stocks, health care companies, and some index funds that track the whole market. Each one reacts differently to the economy, so your portfolio won't be wiped out by a sudden crash in one area.

What's even better is to start small and be consistent. It's not about how much money you put in all at once; it's about how often you add to your portfolio. Even investing $10 every month starts the habit and allows your money to grow steadily over time. This habit is usually known as "dollar-cost averaging." Buying small amounts regularly helps you avoid trying to time the market, which is super hard—even for experts.

Another important part is knowing when and how to adjust your portfolio. Let's say you started with mostly stocks when you were 14 because you wanted to grow your money aggressively for college in 6 years. But now, at 17, college is just around the corner, and you want to avoid big losses. This means shifting some of your money from stocks to safer investments like bonds or a high-yield savings account. It's like slowly changing the settings on your music playlist to match your mood. You want to protect the progress you've made so far.

But don't stress if you don't get this perfect right away. Portfolio building is a learning process. Keep an eye on how your investments are doing, but try not to obsess over daily changes. The market will go up and down—this is normal. What matters most is the long-term trend.

One way to keep your portfolio growing with you is to think about your personal goals and timeline. When do you want to buy something big, like a car, or start a business? When might you want to take a gap year abroad? The answers help you figure out how much risk makes sense. If something is happening soon, you don't want your entire portfolio tied up in risky stocks that could drop overnight. But if it's something ten years away, you can handle more ups and downs because time is on your side.

As you get older and your income grows—from part-time jobs, babysitting gigs, or even your own side hustle—you can add more complexity to your portfolio. That might mean looking into real estate, mutual funds, or even starting a small business that earns money and grows in value. Your portfolio isn't just stocks and bonds; it's everything you own that can increase your wealth.

Another tip is to educate yourself constantly. Markets change, new products pop up, and your financial situation changes too. There's no shame in asking for help—from parents, mentors, or financial advisors—especially as your portfolio grows larger. Just remember, no one knows exactly what will happen tomorrow, so don't follow tips blindly. Getting comfortable with your own knowledge and judgement is what helps make smart decisions.

Technology today offers powerful tools that teens didn't have a decade ago. You can use apps that let you track your portfolio, learn about investments, and even practice trading with virtual money. These tools are fantastic for gaining confidence without risking anything. Treat them like a video game challenge or a puzzle you want to solve. The more you play and learn, the better you get at managing your real money later on.

Finally, patience is your best friend. Growing a portfolio isn't about instant riches; it's about steady, steady progress that rewards you over years and decades. Even if you start with just a little money, the habits and knowledge you build now will give you a huge advantage throughout your adult life. Imagine looking back when you're 30 and realizing you've had money working for you since your teens—that's powerful.

So here's the bottom line: build a portfolio that matches your life, your goals, and your risks. Keep it diversified, stay consistent in your investments, and adjust the mix as your needs change. Most importantly, keep learning and growing. Your portfolio isn't just about money—it's a tool for your future freedom and independence. You've got time on your side, so start now and watch how it grows with you.

WHAT TO DO WHEN THE MARKET DROPS: STRATEGIES FOR TEENS

So, you've started investing, and you're watching your portfolio grow. Life's looking good, right? But then, reality hits—the market takes a tumble. Suddenly, your investments lose value, and panic can set in. That's totally normal, especially when you're just getting started. Understanding how to handle these market drops is a crucial skill for any investor, and it's one that can set you apart from the crowd if you learn it early.

First, let's get one thing straight: the stock market doesn't move in a straight upward line. It's like a roller coaster with ups and downs, twists and turns. When the market drops, it can feel like your money is disappearing, but the truth is, those losses often don't mean much in the long term. What you're seeing is more like a temporary snapshot—not the entire story.

Here's the deal. When the market drops, the best thing you can do is avoid freaking out. Emotional decisions are usually the worst kind in investing. It's tempting to sell everything and run for the hills, especially if you know someone who's losing money too. But if you sell when prices are low, you lock in your losses. Instead, try to keep your cool, take a step back, and remind yourself why you started investing in the first place.

One powerful strategy is to see market drops as opportunities. If your investment goals are long-term, like

106

buying a car, going to college, or building wealth for your future, then downturns can actually be great moments to put more money into investing. When stock prices fall, you can buy shares at a discount. Over time, as the market recovers (and it almost always does), those investments tend to grow significantly.

You might hear adults say things like "buy low, sell high"—and while that sounds simple, it's really hard to execute perfectly. But buying when the market drops gives you a leg up because you're investing in quality companies or funds at cheaper prices. It's like shopping during a sale instead of paying full price later. For teens who have the advantage of time, using market drops wisely can be a game-changer.

But what if you don't have extra money to invest right now? That's okay. Not having cash on hand to invest during a market drop doesn't mean you're out of the game. The most important thing is to stay consistent with whatever amount you can save and invest regularly. This approach is called "dollar-cost averaging," where you invest a fixed amount over time regardless of the market's ups and downs. This strategy helps smooth out your purchase price and reduces the risk of investing a lump sum right before a crash.

Another key mindset is remembering that your investments represent ownership in companies—not just numbers on a screen. When the market dips, you're not losing money in a vacuum; you're temporarily seeing a decline in the value of your shares. The companies still exist, still have products, and often still make money. If you choose solid investments with good fundamentals, they're likely to bounce back eventually.

Where do you start when trying to keep calm during volatile times? Start by having a plan. When you first put together your investment strategy—usually in the "How to Build a Portfolio That Grows with You" section—you should also figure out what you'll do if the market drops by 10%, 20%, or even more. Setting these expectations in advance can keep you from making knee-jerk decisions fueled by fear.

It helps too to remind yourself that the market has survived dozens of crashes and recessions over the past century. Each dip was followed by a period of growth. If you studied just the history of the market, you'd see that fear is one of the biggest traps for investors. Staying confident and patient can be your secret weapon. Developing mental toughness is just as important as learning how to pick stocks or use investing apps.

Sometimes when investing feels scary, it's because you don't fully understand what's happening. So, take the time to learn about the reasons behind market drops. For example, sometimes global events, government policies, or company-specific news cause stocks to dip. But these effects are often short-term. Knowing this can help you see the bigger picture.

For teens, it's also a good moment to lean on a trusted adult mentor, whether that's a parent, teacher, or family friend who knows about investing. Talking things

108

through with someone experienced can provide perspective and reduce anxiety. If you don't have someone in your life who knows investing, consider online communities or forums where you can ask questions and get real, sensible advice.

Now, what about your emotions? It's easy to get caught up in stories from social media or news headlines screaming about crashes and doom. But remember: not all information online is reliable. Avoid the trap of "checking your portfolio every five minutes"—this rarely helps and often makes things worse. Instead, set regular times to review your investments, like once a month or once a quarter, and try to resist the urge to react to short-term market swings.

One more thing: remember to focus on your goals beyond just the market numbers. Your investment journey is part of a larger picture—building security, freedom, and opportunities for your future self. Every dip is a test of patience and discipline. The teens who succeed in investing aren't necessarily the ones who get rich quick but the ones who stick with it through thick and thin.

When the market dips, think of it like training for a sport or learning an instrument. It's the rough patches that help you grow stronger. Building wealth takes time, and setbacks are part of the process. Instead of letting fear take over, use downturns as learning moments. Keep your confidence high and your strategy steady.

To sum up, when the market drops, don't panic. Use the opportunity to buy more if you can. Stick to your investment plan and avoid emotional decisions. Remember the bigger picture and keep learning along the way. By mastering these strategies now, you're setting yourself up to build real wealth over time.

After all, investing isn't about timing every single market move perfectly—it's about staying in the game long enough to see your efforts pay off. Market drops aren't the end; they're just part of the ride. And since you're starting young, you've got one huge advantage: time. A little patience goes a long way.

FINANCIAL FREEDOM: WHAT IT MEANS AND HOW TEENS CAN GET THERE

Financial freedom is a phrase you probably hear a lot, but what does it actually mean? At its core, financial freedom means having enough money saved, invested, and growing so that you don't have to stress about paying bills or making ends meet. It's about having control over your money instead of your money controlling you. For teens, this idea might seem far off or even impossible, but the truth is it's something you can start working towards right now— even before you graduate high school.

Imagine waking up each day without worrying if you're going to run out of money or being forced into a job you hate just to pay rent. That's a glimpse of what financial freedom feels like: being able to make choices based on what you want, not what you need. It's having the freedom to spend time with friends, travel, explore new passions, or even start your own business without constantly stressing about money.

But here's the catch: financial freedom doesn't come from luck or winning the lottery. It comes from habits, knowledge, and most importantly, starting early. When you start building wealth as a teenager, you have one huge advantage—time. Time on your side means your money has a chance to grow and multiply, often in ways that surprise people who wait until they're older to start getting serious about their finances.

Reaching financial freedom is like taking a road trip. You can't just jump in the car and expect to be there instantly—you need a plan, a destination, and some pit stops along the way. For teens, this means learning to manage money well, developing smart saving habits, understanding how to invest, and keeping your eyes open for opportunities that can accelerate your journey. Each smart decision you make now is a mile closer to financial freedom.

Some people think financial freedom means becoming rich overnight. That's a myth. Instead, it's about steady progress—building a strong foundation with every dollar you save, invest, or earn. It's not always about how much your income is but how well you handle the money you do have. You can start by asking yourself simple questions like: "What do I want my money to do for me?" and "How can I make my money work harder?" These questions help shift your mindset from just earning to truly growing your wealth.

Another important part of financial freedom is reducing debt. While many adults struggle with credit card debt, loans, or other financial obligations, you have the chance to avoid unnecessary debt from the start. That means not relying on credit cards without understanding them, not spending more than you earn, and being thoughtful about when and why you borrow money. The less debt you have—or better yet, if you don't have any debt—the easier it is to build real financial freedom.

One common mistake teens make is thinking saving money is boring or unnecessary when you're young. But here's a little secret: even a small amount saved consistently over time can turn into a powerful tool. Think of your money like seeds. The earlier you plant them, the bigger the tree grows. If you can save and invest some of your income—even if it's just a few dollars here and there—it sets you up to have options in the future that others might not. That could be buying a car, paying for college without loans, or investing in a business.

Starting early also means you get to practice patience and discipline. Those are two of the most valuable skills for anyone who wants to reach financial freedom. You'll face temptations to spend money on things that don't last or don't bring real value. Learning to say no, setting limits, and sticking to your financial goals will help you avoid regret later on. When you see other people making poor money choices and struggling, you'll understand how important good habits really are.

Achieving financial freedom doesn't have to be boring either. You can make money management fun and rewarding by setting goals that excite you—like saving up for a concert, a laptop for school, or even your first investment. When you hit those milestones, you build confidence and motivation to keep going. Goals give your financial plan purpose and keep you focused, even when things get tough.

Another key to the journey is education. The more you understand about how money works, how investments grow, and how businesses make money, the better decisions you'll make. You don't need a degree in economics or a finance certification to get started. You just need a willingness to learn, ask questions, and pay attention to how your money moves. Now is the perfect time to soak up knowledge— not just from books but from the real-world experiences of people around you and trustworthy resources online.

It can also be inspiring to remind yourself that you're in a unique position. Many adults wish they'd started managing their money as young as you can. You have access to apps, tools, and platforms that make investing and tracking finances easier than ever. You don't need a ton of money to begin investing or make your first saving goal. The first step is often the hardest, but it's also the most crucial.

When teens begin to understand what financial freedom looks like, it often sparks new ideas and possibilities. Suddenly, money isn't just about spending or saving—it's about creating a lifestyle and future on your own terms. It becomes less scary because you realize you can take control.

The sooner you start, the sooner your money can grow for you, creating options and opportunities that might seem impossible right now but are totally achievable with patience and smart action.

This road to freedom also requires balance. It's great to think long-term, but it's also important to enjoy your life today. That means budgeting to save and invest without feeling deprived. It means recognizing that financial freedom is a journey, not a single destination. Sometimes you'll hit bumps, and that's okay. What matters is that you keep moving forward and adjusting your plan as you learn and grow.

In the end, financial freedom for teens isn't just about money. It's about building confidence, independence, and resilience. It's about knowing you have the power to create a life where money supports your dreams rather than limiting them. And when you commit to that path now, you're setting yourself up for a future where you don't have to worry about money the way many adults do—a future where you call the shots, live with intention, and enjoy financial peace of mind.

Getting to financial freedom might seem like a big deal right now, but it's really just a series of everyday choices built on good habits. Starting small, learning consistently, staying patient, and staying focused will get you there. So take that first step today. Your future self will thank you.

PLANNING YOUR 20S, 30S, AND BEYOND— STARTING TODAY

It might feel a little early to be thinking about your 20s, 30s, and beyond when you're still in your teens. But the truth is, the choices you make right now can set the foundation for a future where money works for you, not the other way around. Imagine your financial life as a road trip. The earlier you start mapping your route, the smoother and more enjoyable your journey will be. This means you don't have to scramble or feel overwhelmed when you hit major milestones like college, a first job, or buying your own place.

Here's the deal: wealth building isn't just about having a fat bank account. It's about building habits and setting yourself up with a mindset that keeps you growing, no matter what comes your way. You're learning how to do that right this second, so why not apply it to the long game? When you start thinking about your financial future as a series of stages instead of one big "someday," it's easier to stay on track without feeling like you're missing out today.

In your 20s, things are likely to feel pretty exciting and maybe a little unpredictable. Maybe you're heading off to college, starting your first real job, or even traveling somewhere new. It's a time full of possibility, but also a lot of expenses that can pile up fast—think rent, textbooks, groceries, maybe even paying back some student loans. This decade is also where you have the greatest advantage, thanks to time. You've got decades ahead to let your investments grow, so starting early can completely change the game for you.

But "starting early" doesn't mean putting everything you have into complicated investments right away. It means building a solid base—like continuing to save, learning how to budget with your changing lifestyle, and getting comfortable making financial decisions that feel right for you. This is your chance to get familiar with managing money on your own terms. Whenever you can, put away even small amounts of money regularly because that consistency is powerful. The magic of compound interest waits for no one, and your 20s are prime years to let it work its magic.

Moving into your 30s, it's common for things to look a bit different. Maybe your income has grown, or you've taken on bigger responsibilities like a family or a mortgage. This decade is where you're often balancing all kinds of financial priorities—saving for emergencies, thinking about retirement, and maybe even investing more aggressively. If you've done some groundwork in your 20s, this becomes much easier. The habits you develop now don't just set you up to have more money—they help you feel confident and in control of your financial future.

By the time you reach your 30s, your financial goals might start shifting, but that's totally normal. What you want in life today might look very different from your plans five or ten years from now, and your roadmap needs to be flexible. The key is knowing how to adjust without losing momentum. Sticking to your core goals, whether that's

116

building a solid emergency fund or growing your investment portfolio, gives you a steady base to work from even if your path takes unexpected turns.

You can think of your wealth-building journey as a marathon, not a sprint—but it's a marathon where every step counts. Setting smart goals—whether small weekly savings goals or bigger targets like buying a car or starting a business—keeps things moving forward. Some goals might be just a few years away, while others stretch decades into the future. The best part? Goals can evolve, and reviewing your plan regularly makes sure you're always steering in the right direction.

Another important piece of the puzzle: financial knowledge. As you get older, you'll dive deeper into different ways to grow your money, like stocks, bonds, real estate, or even entrepreneurship. But the really smart move is using your early years to practice good money habits. When you truly understand how money flows in and out of your life, the strategies you learn later will be easier to grasp and apply. Plus, nurturing curiosity about finance and investing now means you won't be intimidated when opportunities come knocking.

It's also worth mentioning mindset again—because your attitude about money can be a huge game-changer. Some people grow up thinking money is scary or only for certain "types" of people. You have a chance to rewrite that narrative. Seeing money management as a tool for freedom and possibility will keep you motivated. It makes the whole process less about restrictions and more about choices. When you choose to invest in yourself and your future, you're planting seeds that will grow into much bigger things later.

What about the stuff you'll learn in other parts of this book? This section isn't about the nuts and bolts of investing or budgeting—that's coming up. Instead, it's about looking at your life like a financial planner might—anticipating the changes ahead and knowing you have what it takes to adapt. By thinking about your financial life in stages, you're less likely to get overwhelmed or procrastinate. You're creating a rhythm that fits your unique pace and plans.

Don't forget: life throws curveballs. Jobs change, expenses pop up unexpectedly, and sometimes the market will dip. But when you've planned ahead, these challenges don't knock you down. They become opportunities to learn and adjust. Keeping an emergency fund, continuing education about money, and leaning on trusted advice when you need it keeps your roadmap flexible and resilient.

One final thought: sharing your financial journey with others can be surprisingly helpful. It might feel awkward to talk about money at first, but opening up to friends, family, or mentors creates a support system. You're not the only one figuring this out, and sometimes hearing how others handle their 20s or 30s financially can give you fresh ideas or boost your confidence. Remember, building wealth isn't just about numbers—it's about building your whole life in a way that feels right for you.

118

So, to sum it all up—start today by imagining where you want to be in 10, 20, or even 30 years. Think about what kind of financial habits you need to build to get there, and commit to learning and growing bit by bit. Your 20s and 30s will fly by faster than you think, but if you begin planning now, you'll be amazed at how strong and steady your financial future becomes.

CONCLUSION

Wrapping all this up, it's clear that starting your financial journey early isn't just a good idea—it's the smartest move you can make to set yourself up for life. The earlier you get comfortable with money, investing, and smart habits, the more time your wealth has to grow and work for you. It's not about having a ton of cash right off the bat; it's about building momentum, learning along the way, and staying consistent. Small steps, repeated over time, create big results.

What's really exciting is that the power to shape your financial future is in your hands, and you don't have to wait until you're an adult or have a high-paying job to begin. Every dollar you save, every investment you make—no matter how modest—gets you that much closer to financial independence. Think of it like planting a tree. The earlier you plant it, the bigger and stronger it grows. Your money tree is your investments and habits, nurtured by knowledge and action every day.

Of course, this journey isn't without bumps. There will be times when the market dips, or when you feel like giving up because saving seems too hard or dashed dreams get in your way. That's normal. What sets successful young investors apart is the mindset to keep going, to keep learning, and to view mistakes as lessons rather than failures. Resilience is a huge part of building wealth, so don't let short-term obstacles derail the long game.

Remember, investing is more than just numbers and charts—it's about your future dreams. Whether you want to travel, start a business, go to college without debt, or just have the freedom to choose what you do with your time, money is the tool that helps make those dreams a reality. When you understand that, saving and investing don't feel like chores; they become exciting steps toward turning your vision into a plan you can follow.

It's also crucial to remember that building wealth isn't about keeping score with your friends or competing to look richer. It's a personal challenge and a way to ensure your security and freedom. Money isn't a goal by itself—it's a means to live the kind of life you want, without worry or limits. Aligning your financial habits with your values and goals gives those dollars purpose and meaning.

The knowledge you've gained here—about money basics, investing concepts, smart habits, and setting up your financial roadmap—is your launchpad. Use it. Make mistakes, but make them informed. Ask questions, stay curious, and keep pushing yourself. The world of finance can seem intimidating, but it's full of opportunity for anyone willing to learn and take action.

Besides, it's not magic or luck that makes people wealthy—it's discipline, patience, curiosity, and sometimes a little creativity. Those are things you already have or can develop. Every lesson you learn now builds a foundation for bigger wins in the years ahead. Once you get that confidence, managing money shifts from overwhelming to empowering.

Finally, don't forget the value of sharing what you learn. Talk with friends or family about money, help each other stay accountable to saving and investing goals, and watch as your collective knowledge grows. Financial skills aren't just for individuals; they strengthen communities and give everyone a better shot at success. You could be the spark that sets off financial confidence in those around you.

In the end, growing your wealth isn't about being perfect—it's about being proactive. Start now, start small, but start. The power of compound interest, the benefit of informed choices, and the strength of a resilient mindset will carry you further than you ever expect. You've got a head start on a future filled with possibilities. Use it well.

APPENDIX: ADDITIONAL RESOURCES FOR TEEN INVESTORS

So, you've got the basics down, and you're ready to take your investing journey even further. That's where this section comes in. Think of it as your go-to toolkit packed with extra resources that'll help you stay sharp, learn new moves, and keep your money game strong.

First off, there are tons of websites designed specifically for teens wanting to learn about money and investing. They break down complicated stuff into bite-sized pieces that actually make sense. Some even offer simulation games where you can practice investing without risking real cash. This is a fantastic way to build confidence before jumping in with your own money.

Podcasts and YouTube channels are also a goldmine. Listening to successful investors talk about their wins, losses, and lessons can give you fresh perspectives and real-world insights. Plus, you can tune in while on the go, whether you're walking home from school or helping out around the house.

Don't overlook books—some are written just for young people like you and answer questions you didn't even know you had. They can serve as both inspiration and a roadmap to smarter investing habits. The key is finding authors who explain things clearly without treating you like a novice—or talking down to you.

Apps aren't just for fun or social media; many are created with teens in mind to help manage money, track spending, and even invest small amounts. Choosing the right one can simplify things and help you build good financial habits early on.

And lastly, look for local or online groups where teens interested in investing hang out. Community support makes a huge difference—being able to ask questions, share wins, and even talk through setbacks keeps motivation high. Plus, networking early can open doors down the road.

WHERE TO START

1. **Educational Websites** — Find pages that focus on teen investing and money basics. They're usually updated with the latest tips and trends.

2. **Podcasts & Webinars** — Subscribe to a couple that resonate with you, and listen regularly to build your knowledge.

3. **Books for Young Investors** — Pick titles aimed at your age group that cover investing fundamentals and success stories.

4. **Investment Apps** — Try beginner-friendly platforms that allow small investments and offer educational content.

5. **Youth Investment Clubs** — Join or start one in your school or community to connect with peers who share your financial goals.

Remember, learning about investing and money management is a lifelong journey. The resources here are just a starting point to empower you to make decisions with confidence. Keep exploring, stay curious, and don't be afraid to dive into new topics as you go. Your future self will thank you.

www.ingramcontent.com/pod-product-compliance
Lightning Source LLC
Chambersburg PA
CBHW030944090426
42737CB00007B/528